THE
STOCK MARKET
EXPLAINED

Your Guide to Successful Investing

Alvin Hall

**HODDER &
STOUGHTON**

First published in Great Britain in 2012 by Hodder & Stoughton
An Hachette UK company

1

Copyright © Alvin Hall 2012

The right of Alvin Hall to be identified as the Author of the
Work has been asserted by him in accordance with the Copyright,
Designs and Patents Act 1988.

A CIP catalogue record for this title is available from the British Library

ISBN 978 1 444 72017 4
eBook ISBN 978 1 444 72018 1

Printed and bound by Clays Ltd, St Ives plc

Hodder & Stoughton policy is to use papers that are natural,
renewable and recyclable products and made from wood grown
in sustainable forests. The logging and manufacturing processes
are expected to conform to the environmental regulations
of the country of origin.

Hodder & Stoughton Ltd
338 Euston Road
London NW1 3BH

www.hodder.co.uk

THE
STOCK MARKET
EXPLAINED

Alvin Hall is an internationally renowned financial educator, television and radio broadcaster, bestselling author, and regular contributor to magazines, newspapers, and websites. For five years on the BBC, he hosted the highly rated and award-winning series, *Your Money or Your Life*, on which he offered both practical financial and psychological advice to people about how to take control of and fix their financial problems. Hall lives in New York City where he designs and teaches classes about the investment markets for financial services companies, banks, regulatory authorities, as well as information and technology vendors.

To Leo, Leona, and Ed
for hiring me for my first job in the financial markets

CONTENTS

Acknowledgements

Since starting on Wall Street on 7 December 1982 as a director of course development for a training company, I have never lost my interest in the financial markets, especially the way they work, the similarities and differences among countries, and their continual evolution, often in unpredictable ways. For me, this means I'm never bored. There's always the challenge and anxiety of learning something new and then figuring out ways to teach and explain the information or process to others.

This book is specifically about the stock market in the United Kingdom. Writing it required me to continually shift between being a student (learning some totally different procedures and terminology), being a teacher figuring out the best way to present what I've learned and not evoke the 'glaze over' factor), and being a writer (trying to remain aware of the needs and anticipate the questions of the proverbial 'reader over my shoulder').

I thank the following people for their support and contributions: Roger Bakeman, Ciara Foley, Mick Gilligan, Patrick Gordon, Christian Hobart, Penny Isaac, Paul Killik, Ian-Patrick Lauder, Vicki McIvor, Mark Montgomery, Sophie Morris, Van Morrow, Sarah Pennells, Eric Raphael, Xavier Rolet, Mike Savage, Allen Simpson, Kimberlee Sheldon, Rowena Webb and Karl Weber. And I thank my students – the people who have attended and continue to attend my training classes for various companies. The questions they ask during these sessions as well as the looks on their faces let me know immediately and in person when they are connecting the dots and understanding the information, or glazing over because I've become pedantic and dull. All of this helps me to continue developing effective, engaging ways of communicating the information in the book.

FOREWORD

Xavier Rolet
Chief Executive, London Stock Exchange Group

The first shares were sold in 1553, half a mile from the modern-day location of the London Stock Exchange in the heart of the City of London. The money invested was to fund an exploration business called, quite exotically, the *Company of Merchant Adventurers to New Lands*.

That same year, three of the Company's ships set sail in search of the Northeast Passage to China. As with many new ventures, not all went according to plan. One of the ships was lost en route and another froze off the coast of northern Scandinavia. Investors may have thought that was the last they had seen of their money, but the last ship met with far better fortunes. The ship's crew initially docked in Russia and then travelled on through 600 miles of ice-covered waterway to reach Moscow. Returning to England a year later, they were laden with treasures – gifts from the Czar of Muscovy, furs from the continent and a Royal Charter from the Czar warmly inviting more English traders to Moscow – this was a huge new market for English wool. The Company was rewarded by the Crown with an exclusive right over English-Russian trade that was to last over a hundred years. The Crown was no doubt delighted with the new trade link, the Company's future had been secured and the business's shareholders had become very, very rich.

Importantly, the Merchant Adventurer's success spurred others on to create new merchant joint-stock companies – including the Levant Company (for trade with Turkey) in 1581; the East India Company (India and the East Indies) in 1600; and the Virginia Company (with the new settlements of North America) in 1609. Some of these new ventures met with astonishing success, forming partnerships and relationships across the world that laid the foundations for today's global network of international trade. This in many ways was the birth of today's modern capital markets.

Five hundred years on and the world has radically changed. Capital markets are barely recognisable from a decade ago, let alone from half a millennium. Yet the fundamental principles of investing remain the same. Companies need good capital to grow, innovate and succeed. And if investors plan, take time to understand the dynamics of business, the behaviours of the market place, have passion and a healthy respect for risk, then the opportunities exist for great success on the Stock Market.

Alvin's latest work successfully identifies and explains some of these core principles of good investment decisions. It is a great addition to the literature available on how to successfully manage a portfolio of investments.

It is easy for investors to become overwhelmed by the sheer complexity and scale of financial markets: a book like this helps de-mystify the jargon and makes the world of investing accessible.

Alvin's strength lies in his unique ability to make things clear – introducing equities, fixed income and fund investments through risk and return, the cornerstones of investment theory. His proficiency in making the reader comfortable with the material is marked, and his accessible approach and reader-friendly-style is refreshing.

Financial markets continue to have an incredibly important role to play in the health of our economy as well as for us as individuals: they provide the funding that allows businesses to grow, to create jobs, to be successful. With approximately $60 trillion traded annually on equity markets alone, plus the vast array of debt, derivatives and other investment vehicles out there, there is something in the investment world for everyone. Books such as Alvin's can only help investors, beginners and experts alike, make informed and educated investment decisions, and that is a good thing. And, who knows, it may even help you find a 21st century *Company of Merchant Adventurers to New Lands.*

INTRODUCTION

Let's begin with what this book is about: 1) *What is a stock exchange?*, and 2) *What is its primary purpose in our lives – whether we invest or whether we are just curious about how investing works?*

One of the objectives of **The Stock Market Explained** is to provide you with essential classic and timeless information about the market. With this knowledge, you can, as I did, decide how to use it in ways that are appropriate for you, as one of the tools to accumulate the financial security you desire.

Money and the stock market were not subjects I was naturally interested in. Arts and literature spoke (and still speak) to my soul. However, I discovered, much to my surprise, that money and stock markets were more creative and exciting than I could have imagined. I began working in the financial markets on 7 December 1982, with one goal in mind: to learn how money works. I had little money at that time – less than the equivalent of a thousand pounds in a savings account. However, some of the people I had gone to college with were multimillionaires. One was rumoured to be on his way to becoming a billionaire. Looking at my own financial situation, I could not help but wonder what these once-fellow students knew about money that I did not or had missed learning. Was there a secret that I had not been told about? It became my quiet, personal goal to find out.

Making money for myself was not my goal – yet. I was happy and inspired learning the information through reading books and having insightful conversations with long-time practitioners (the proverbial 'good ol' boys'). This knowledge enabled me to write training manuals and then books for people entering the financial services industry that explained the basics of ordinary shares, preference shares, money-market securities, corporate bonds, futures, options, trading, investment analysis and the economic cycles, among many other topics. I think what excited me most, and overrode any anxiety I had about studying these sometimes complex subjects, was the discovery that there was a lot more creativity in the financial markets than I could ever have imagined. There would always be something new to learn, which meant I was unlikely to get bored.

Soon I had learned enough to be able to teach classes about investment products and their markets. Curiously, I did not attach this investment knowledge to my own financial goals – which I had yet to clearly formulate. I'm sure that I assumed I would work for a company that would pay me a salary, match my regular contributions to a pension or retirement plan, offer me domestic and international career growth, and give me an appropriate cash bonus or gift upon my retirement. It wasn't until about three years after I started teaching classes on Wall Street that it dawned on me (like an Oprah 'ah-ha moment') that I probably understood enough to invest the money I had earned and saved. After all, I was teaching this information to others – quite effectively.

My first experiences in investing – which ranged from

amazingly good to truly naïve and depressing – deepened my understanding of and wisdom about the markets. Although I lost quite a bit of my hard-earned money in my first attempts at investing, I did not become afraid of the markets. I did, however, develop a healthy sense of scepticism and an understanding of the need to base my decisions on quality information and to control my expectations. Surprisingly, my experiences actually increased my curiosity and my resolve to make investing work for me. Without immediately realising it, I had learned one of the key lessons about the stock market and investing: one must always remain a student of the investment markets in order to make more informed and more insightful investment decisions over time.

I developed my own simple, patient approach to selecting securities in which to invest. I did not look for any 'secret' strategies. I did not feel the need to act like a trader or to show how smart I was about investing. The money I made was my own private accomplishment – and it gave me an unexpected sense of contentment. Importantly, from all of my experiences I realised I had gained the 'missed knowledge' about money that started my journey (another Oprah 'ah-ha moment'). I'll share with you the simple principles of that knowledge at various times throughout this book.

The ever-changing nature of my work made a huge contribution to my knowledge about money and investing. Developing courses for and teaching about the financial markets also proved to be an unexpected pleasure. Because I found the information interesting and exciting, I tried to impart this in the way I taught the different subjects in my training sessions, as well as how I wrote about them in books and articles.

For many people – from cab drivers I talked to on my way to do interviews for this book, to people sitting next to me on flights where I was editing the manuscript, to friends and acquaintances who were curious about my next book project – the term 'the stock market' evokes a singularly raucous and mystifying image. Most people immediately envision wildly animated groups of traders, dressed in suits, standing in a crowded room (known as a *trading floor*), shouting out the prices at which they want to either buy (*bid prices*) or sell (*offer prices*) a quantity of *stocks* or *shares*, while simultaneously using special hand signals to repeat and confirm those bids and offers. Scenes like this took place when each trader 'owned a seat' or worked for a brokerage firm that owned one (or more). This ownership, which was another term for being a member in good standing of a specific stock exchange, gave the traders the exclusive right to execute orders on behalf of themselves and others for all stocks and shares that were 'listed' (authorised to trade by the stock exchange) on that specific trading floor.

Today, most traditional trading floors have been consolidated, downsized, or closed, replaced with computerised trading platforms. Many exchanges have changed from member-only or mutual organisations to for-profit corporations, which have responsibilities to their shareholders. While some markets like the New York Stock Exchange and the Tokyo Stock Exchange still maintain traditional trading floors, there is little human involvement in the execution of the majority of orders to trade shares, bonds, and other investment products today. Most of the buying and selling of *securities* – the group name for all investment products (shares, bonds, investment trusts, unit trusts, exchange-traded funds, options, etc.) that are listed and traded on a stock exchange or other type of stock market – is now done electronically, via high-speed computers that automatically match trades or find the appropriate opposite side. For example, if you enter an order to buy securities, a computer-driven order-execution system finds an appropriate seller at the price at which you are willing to pay, or lower. Today, what we think of as a stock exchange (which is also referred to as a *market centre* or a *pool of liquidity*) can be 'any organisation, association, or group of persons that (1) bring together the orders of multiple buyers and sellers, and (2) use established, non-discretionary methods (whether by providing a trading facility or setting rules) under which such orders interact with each other, and the buyers and sellers entering such orders agree to the terms of the trade.'* This new, expanded definition of a stock exchange has led to the development of multiple alternative trading venues or market centres in cyberspace, where a customer's order can be executed among computers. A physical location is no longer required and is often thought to be too costly to maintain.

While an exchange's responsibility to provide a physical facility for trading may have changed from an actual floor or room to a virtual one, its other major role in business and the economy remains the same. A stock exchange has been and remains a place where businesses, governments or other organisations seeking to raise capital go to find institutions and individuals

---

* The Regulation of Exchanges and Alternative Trading Systems (commonly referred to as Reg ATS) of the US Securities and Exchange Commission Legislation

willing to invest money in these enterprises in exchange for securities. These might be in the form of shares representing partial ownership in the business, or bonds denoting a loan to the enterprise or organisation. When buying a company's shares, an investor hopes to make back at least the cost of the shares and any amount their market value may increase beyond the price paid. And shareholders also hope to receive periodic *dividends* (a share of a business's profits), which the company's board may decide to pay out. When buying a business's or a government's bonds, the investor expects to receive regular interest payments for a fixed period of time and then be repaid the face value of the bond.

It's important to note here that I use the word 'investor'. Enterprises want to find people who are willing to leave their money in the business or organisation for the long term, thereby allowing the management time to focus on growing the business. Of course, not all people who buy stocks and shares are interested in the long-term growth of the business enterprise. You might want to make a quick return and move on to the next moneymaking opportunity. This quick, short-term trading is called *speculation*. It is not the same as investing. In fact, some people might say it's contrary to investing, but it is an important aspect of the stock market nonetheless. Speculators, with their quick buying and selling, add liquidity to the markets, thus making it easy for others (investors and other speculators) to buy stock and bonds, as well as to sell (i.e. *liquidate*) them when they want to.

Both investing and speculating involve risk. If the business or entity performs poorly or fails, or a government defaults on its debt, then you, the investor or speculator, could lose all or part of the money that used to buy the securities of that entity. Every year hundreds of companies around the world 'go public', or issue more securities on the stock exchanges, in order to gain access to investors – preferably long-term investors – willing to accept the risks of losing the money they've invested in exchange for the potential financial rewards: capital appreciation, dividend payments, or interest payments.

Not all people have a positive or neutral view of a stock exchange as simply a place where people buy and sell stocks and shares. A few people offer a more cynical description: 'It's a licensed casino for gambling where the majority of people lose money because the odds are stacked against them.' In truth, this comparison is flawed. Casino gambling is a zero-sum game – i.e. for every winner there is a loser; in investing this is not true. When a stock rises, everyone who owns it makes money. However, given the scandals (both historic and present), as well as the headline, minute-by-minute coverage that the gyrations of the investment markets get on television, radio, the internet and in daily publications, this response is understandable. The daily flow of words and statistics about the financial markets – the number of shares traded, the amount that share prices increase or decrease throughout the day, the percentage of price change compared to the previous day's close, the up or down movement of indices that measure the overall market – certainly seem to support the perceptions that stock markets are places for short-term moneymaking; hence the frequent comparison to a casino. In truth, there is an undeniable titillation to being able to buy and sell shares quickly on a stock exchange or other investment model to potentially make 'fast money'. This approach garners a great deal of attention – and appeals to people's get-rich-quick fantasies. Ultimately, how you choose to use (or not use) your money in the stock market is a decision that you must make for yourself given your financial resources, your risk tolerance, and how directly involved you want to be with your investment decisions.

The Stock Market Explained allows me to blend the two roles that have been central to sustaining my interest and career in the financial markets: being a student and being a teacher. Having now taught about the stock market as well as other investment markets for nearly 30 years, and continuing to do so, I bring to this book the insights gained from thousands of interactive classroom hours spent explaining these concepts to real people. I've used their questions and comments, and the reactions reflected in their eyes, faces and body language to develop, and over time refine, examples, comparisons, analogies, similes and stories that I hope communicate clearly and effectively to the wide range of interests and experiences among people who may read this book.

Keeping you engaged with this information is one of my goals. Many people – from publishers to the average person on the street – prejudge books and articles about finances and investing, concluding confidently that they are always going to be mindnumbingly boring. By the end of this book, I hope you'll find that this is not the case. I hope that the stock market helps you understand other aspects of your own daily interaction with banks and building societies, other businesses, the news, and, perhaps most importantly, your own money and aspirations for financial wellbeing. It may turn out that investing may be something you should not only know something about (as many of us ought to), but should consider for some of your money.

1

THINGS TO CONSIDER
BEFORE YOU INVEST

I was finishing this book during the big market declines and wild volatility of August and September 2011. It was unsettling and scary, even for someone like me who not only invests but who also teaches and writes about the workings of the markets. In an interview a few days before the first big drop, a reporter asked me what would be a good strategy during these uncertain times, if the markets suddenly dropped or became volatile. At the time I'm sure neither of us could have realised the short-term prescience of this question. In my response I embedded another question, one I was trying to answer for myself as I determined what action I was going to take regarding my own investments: Do you want to be safe or do you want to be smart?

I've thought about these choices repeatedly through the wild up-and-down moves of the market throughout late 2011. Without any prompting, friends and acquaintances told me what had happened to their investments – and their nerves – during this volatile period. Their ages ranged from early 20s to mid-70s. Their investment experiences ranged from being totally new ('It was the first time I'd ever put money in the stock market'), to having invested with better-than-average success for four decades or longer. Their understanding of their own risk tolerance has ranged from, 'Oh, I never thought about that' to, 'Experience has taught me to always follow my gut instincts.' Interestingly, their reactions have ranged from full-on regret about their loss (tinged with a little cynicism and anger) to a repeated affirmation (almost mantra-like) of their belief in the long-term, buy-and-hold view of the markets, *à la* Warren Buffett.

Thinking about all I heard, I felt it was important to extract from their (as well as my own) long-time and recent investing experiences the new lessons, wisdoms and insights we had gained. I wanted to include in this first chapter all those that relate to the financial, intellectual and emotional perspectives a person must have about investing. I know – from the many questions I'm asked – that most people want there to be a perfect formula for successful investing. There is none. They also want to find someone (a broker or financial adviser) who will accurately predict and therefore get out of the market before any downturn. Not even long-time gurus can do that through all market conditions. There is no denying the fact that investment markets have changed and will continue to do so in ways that are not always predictable. This is currently indicated by an unusually high volume of trading, as well as an increasing number of purely speculative traders for whom short-term volatility – as opposed to long-term holding – represents a profit opportunity. I would be dishonest if I did not say that the expanding use of high-speed, algorithmic trading will certainly increase the impact of this speculative activity on the markets in the future, most likely increasing volatility.

So how does a retail investor – you and me – go about making money in the stock and bond markets of today and in the future? In a departure from the usual approach of books explaining how the investment markets work, I've decided to begin with what you need to ask yourself and think about carefully about *before* you invest. You may discover that investing or simply understanding the financial markets is something you are interested in. The information in this chapter will help you to clarify *why* you might want to buy shares and bonds. On the other hand, you may discover that investing is not for you. This is totally fine too. It's better to find out beforehand so you don't invest blithely, lose money, and then be filled with distress and regret.

Here are six topics you need to consider – some classic, some new – and have reasonable answers to before you invest. I believe this pre-thinking and pre-planning can serve as a useful guide to investing in the markets today. Importantly, in keeping with the question I mentioned earlier, 'Do you want to be safe or do you want to be smart?', these topics will also help you achieve the right balance between the two choices. And as you think about them more, these subjects will naturally put the brakes on becoming too clever. One should only attempt to be clever when one has investment experience and knowledge, as well as a clear understanding of the increased risk of loss associated with more complicated strategies. And you must be able to withstand the losses financially.

1. Think seriously about your risk tolerance. Can you afford to lose the money or not to have access to it for a while?

This point can never be emphasised enough. All investing involves risk; therefore, you should invest no more money than you can afford to lose. You could lose some or all of the money you have invested in stocks, bonds, unit trusts or other vehicles. Don't fool yourself about this, as many people do every year. They hear the words 'guaranteed' and 'investment' used together and slowly but surely believe they, or someone they've just met, have discovered the secret formula or strategy to a no-lose way to make money. In truth, when you hear this phrase or a similar one related to investments, walk away from the proposition or opportunity. Risk of loss is inherent to all investments. There is no such thing as a risk-free investment.

You must seek to quantify your risk tolerance. A simple way to start the process is to think about how much money you can tolerate losing without it affecting your lifestyle or causing emotional distress. The prices of all securities traded in the financial markets will go up and down. What percentage of loss will leave you in a state of panic or regret: 10%, 20%, 30%? This is something you need to think about seriously before you invest. Only you can set this limit for yourself. In doing so you establish the range of daily price fluctuation that you can tolerate without becoming overly anxious.

Keep in mind that your risk tolerance is always associated with the time horizon of your investment. If you're investing and trying to achieve significant gains over the short-term, then you will be subject to significant risk of loss if the market unexpectedly moves opposite to your expectations. Afterwards, you can only hope (because there is never a guarantee) that the market will recover enough for you to simply break even. This is a truth that many investors, especially those with little or no experience, try to rationalise away, often to their detriment.

In general, the longer your time horizon, the easier

it is to withstand, financially and emotionally, the ups and downs. This is based on the fact that the market has historically moved higher (i.e. been bullish) over the longer term, despite some significant periods when prices and values have declined (i.e. been bearish). That said, it may take the markets a long time to recover from losses. You may end up holding positions for a lot longer than you had initially planned. The bottom-line question related to risk tolerance is, 'Can you afford to *not* have access to your money for a longer-than-expected period of time (if you're waiting for a recovery) or forever (if the investment is a total loss)?' Be as clear and honest as you can.

2. Set your investment objective. Have you decided what you want to achieve as well as how and when you want to achieve it?

It always prompts concern in me when someone says his or her objective is to make money or become rich. I hear an unsettling naivety in this declaration. There are many ways to achieve both in one's life, one's career – and one's fantasies. Successful investing, however, requires a person to define more specific details, such as:

- the reason he or she is investing;
- the time horizon of the investment (such as retirement or the year a child is likely to start university);
- the target amount of money you would like to accumulate over a period of time;
- the strategy (e.g. buy-and-hold, income generation, speculation) he or she understands and is most comfortable using;

5

- the reasonable annual return (given the overall economic conditions);
- the risks he or she is willing to take to achieve the goal.

Being specific helps you in important ways – both practically and psychologically. First, by giving yourself a well-defined goal to achieve, you can set benchmarks that measure your progress toward your goal. You can build in treats for yourself that not only celebrate your achievements but also motivate you to apply even more determination to reach the next benchmark and the next one after that. This can be very gratifying because you are accomplishing this for yourself. Perhaps most importantly, reaching each intermediate goal periodically reminds you of your long-term goal and helps you to keep it clearly (and repeatedly) in focus. And keep in mind a basic truth about investing: growth today leads to higher income in the future.

Psychologically, making your investment objective real and understandable for yourself can increase the likelihood that you will achieve it. You have a target and therefore won't be drifting aimlessly towards some unknown place. Seeing yourself moving closer to achieving your goals helps to reinforce the behaviour – diligence, sacrifice, deferred gratification, and others – that are essential elements of building financial security at all economic and income levels.

3. Set rules for yourself. Can you remain reasonably rational while making financial decisions?

Investing is, for most people, an optimistic endeavour. You buy shares, bonds, or unit trusts believing – wishing and hoping and praying – that the company will grow, the market value of the shares will increase, the company may eventually begin paying dividends to shareholders, and it will be able to make its promised interest payments on its bonds. This optimism must be supported by the reality of the business's profitability and growth prospects. Remaining objective about an investment is one of the keys to controlling risk. When an investor becomes overly emotional about an investment (or, to use a more common phrase, 'becomes married to an investment'), the chances of making a mistake due to a lapse in objective judgement increase.

As an investor, you must be emotionally disciplined with yourself. If you reacted to every rally and decline in the market, or to every rumour of a strong rally or precipitous decline, your trading fees would gobble up your money and your emotional state would be kindly described as manic. Who wants to live like that? One way to add a degree of objectivity to your approach to investing is to establish a firm set of simple, straightforward rules before you put your first penny into the market. These will guide your decisions – i.e. to sell, to hold, to add to a position, to sit on the sidelines and accumulate cash – in particular situations. It may take you a few attempts to come up with your rules and to make sure they don't contradict each other. These rules must remain firmly in place and should not change often. You may refine them at first, but don't make wholesale changes to them unless they have caused you to make a significant mistake. (One always makes mistakes when investing. It's part of the process. Over time you want to make fewer and fewer of them.) Only change a rule if the information you are evaluating changes significantly or when you have enough experience to reasonably and rationally justify a change.

One reason to establish a set of guiding rules is to help you avoid looking back at a financial decision with regret. This 'shoulda, coulda, woulda' emotional state can lead you to make an even bigger mistake, based on a past situation that you might subconsciously be trying to make right. Missed opportunities – especially those when you could have made even more money, or avoided a loss – are where regret is most often focused when it comes to money. It's important to learn from the past, but you must avoid being trapped by it.

Make the best decision with all of the financial information you have at the time and don't second-guess yourself once you've made that decision. Part of being optimistic is to know that there are always new opportunities that will come along; you just don't know when. Glean whatever wisdom you can about yourself, about the investment strategy, or about the workings of the product itself, and use that to make a new and better decision in the future.

4. Do you understand the benefits and limits of diversification?

There are two well-known risks associated with investing in shares and bonds. They are company-specific risk (also called *unsystematic risk*) and market risk (called *systematic risk*). The wild fluctuations in August and September 2011 were textbook examples of market or systematic risk. This is the loss that results when there is a decline in the overall investment markets. Anyone holding a portfolio of stocks watched, in quiet concern and increasing distress, as the value of virtually all the shares they owned decreased in value on certain days. The only way to protect against market risk is by using sophisticated strategies involving *derivatives*, such as index options and futures, to hedge against a decline in the value of the portfolio. [Note: These hedging strategies are complex and require skills and specific types of information that are beyond the intended scope of this book.] Most people respond to market risk by 1) trying to anticipate the decline in order sell their securities before it occurs; or 2) continuing to hold the shares, waiting and hoping for the prices to recover.

Company-specific risk is the risk that all the bonds and shares you own in a company (for example, Lehman Brothers) would suddenly be worth nothing because the company declares bankruptcy, or that the securities' value would drop significantly due to bad news about the company's financial situation or future growth prospects. When this risk affects companies in a specific business group, like the bank shares during the recent financial crisis, it is known as *sector risk*. In order to protect against both of these risks, the age-old advice is to diversify. Importantly, diversification no longer means owning stocks and bonds of companies in different business sectors and with different growth and risk prospects. Today, diversification considers the following asset classes: cash, shares (domestic, international and index), bonds, property, commodities (such as precious metals and heating oil) and other assets. It means 1) owning securities across different business sectors; and 2) owning investments in other asset classes that are appropriate for your risk tolerance.

One key lesson that was reiterated by all investors I

spoke with is that being diversified across asset classes has helped lessen the impact of the recent stock-market decline. Diversification does not mean you won't lose money; instead, you may lose less. Look at the evidence of that. With both share prices and property prices (except for trophy properties) generally down, people have bought bonds (for safety) and precious metals (as an inflation hedge). This increased demand has driven prices higher. Some of the gains in these asset classes will have reduced the losses on an investors' share portfolios.

Having too much money in one asset class is clearly risky – even in property and gold, two asset classes that most people believe never lose value. The outlook for a particular asset class does not remain the same; therefore, the type of diversification that works today may need to be tweaked in response to changing market and economic outlooks for the future. In 2011, for example, diversification would have been less effective in providing as much protection as it has historically. Why? In an unusual market development, there was surprisingly high correlation among the price movements of different asset classes. In short, many of the investments – stocks, bonds, and others – moved in the same direction at the same time. This phenomenon indicated that retail and institution investors were all responding to the economic and market uncertainties in the same ways: buying on positive news and selling on bad news regardless of the asset class. As a result, investors felt like they had all of their eggs in one basket despite being diversified. Understanding such situations and being flexible in your investment approach can increase the possibility that you will be successful, as market conditions inevitably change.

5. Set up regular periodic reviews and make appropriate adjustments.

Many people want investing to be like the Sleeping Beauty fairy tale. You put your money in the market with the right financial professional (a stockbroker or financial adviser), you go to sleep leaving them to do their job, and at retirement you wake up to find your broker or adviser delivering to you more financial security (i.e. total net worth) than you could have imagined. If only investing in the stock market really worked like that!

Successful investing depends on you, the investor, participating in the process. If you're an active trader, buying and selling on your own, then this is obviously the case. But when your investments are being managed or directed by a professional, your involvement remains as important, if less frequent.

Set up a regular set of appointments with your broker or financial adviser to:

- review your investments;
- review and compare what has happened with your holdings and the overall market since your last meeting;
- determine if they are on course to achieve your investment objective;
- understand what your broker or financial adviser foresees about the market performance over the next quarter or six months;
- talk with him or her about your thoughts regarding the market, as well as any changes in your personal situations (such as marriage, birth of a child, increased expenses, reduction or loss of income, inheritance, divorce);

- refine or change your holdings to reflect any changes in your life, risk tolerance, or view about the market;
- make him or her aware of any areas of the market that are of special interest to you;
- ask questions about your investments and the overall investment markets.

Getting clear, understandable answers to your questions is one of the reasons for scheduling these periodic meetings. The financial professional you are working with must be able to answer your questions in words and sentences that you can understand.

People tend to treat financial advisers with the deference they accord to a medical professional. However, while they may question their doctors in detail about a particular procedure or medicine if they are not clear about the terminology being used, they often sit defensively and silently in front of their financial adviser, as if he or she is speaking a linguistic equivalent of reverse Polish notation, without asking for explanations. Perhaps part of this comes from our belief that we will ultimately be able to understand medical terminology because it's about something concrete (i.e. our bodies and ourselves), whereas financial terms deal with more abstract concepts related to numbers, notes and value.

Neither medical nor financial information enters our brains via osmosis. There's an understandably natural inclination to do research about issues related to our physical health and wellbeing: think about your online research when your doctor says you have a specific malady. However, there's less of an inclination to do similar research when it relates to investments. Part of the purpose of this book is to help you gain the basic knowledge foundation you need to understand what is being said to you, and to be familiar with the terms you need in order to ask questions appropriate to your financial needs. You don't have to understand every single thing about the markets before your first conversation with a financial adviser or before you make an investment. But you should start the learning process *before* the first meeting and continue to build on it, directed by your needs or interests, through your time in the markets. As a result, each regular meeting will become not only a review of where you are relative to your goal, but a personal indication of the growth of your knowledge and understanding of investing. Thus, you continually increase your likelihood of being successful through changes in your own life and changes in the markets.

6. Don't get greedy. Remember the adage: bulls make money, bears make money, but pigs get slaughtered.

A long-time friend downsized from a substantial home he had lived in for years to an easier-to-maintain flat. He took some of his sizeable profit and invested in what he was convinced would be the next hot wave of stocks, based on what friends in the markets told him. His more prudent financial adviser, believing that the markets might be heading for a rough period, suggested that my friend slowly 'feather' the money into the shares he wanted to buy, rather than investing it all at once. Convinced that he would miss a substantial market rally and the profits it would produce, my friend invested all of the money (and it was not a small amount) in stocks at one time. The market rallied briefly before international concerns caused the stock markets worldwide to post steep declines.

'Remind your readers, up front, not to get greedy, as I did.' This is the before-you-invest advice that this friend strongly suggested I include in this first chapter. He had been investing quite successfully and prudently for decades, and believed he could turn the profits he made from the sale of his property into even bigger profits by investing in what he had been told was the next hot sector. Benjamin Franklin observed that inside every investor is a speculator struggling to get out. My friend's behaviour certainly demonstrates that.

Making fast money is enticing, and certainly gratifying to the ego. But one must remain mindful of the risks associated with trying to substantially outperform the overall market as measured by a benchmark index. It's important to have in mind what is a reasonable return to expect from the markets, and whether your expectations expose you to greater risks than you may have adequately assessed. Know yourself and recognise when the speculator in you is beginning to replace the prudent investor, or when your get-rich-quick fantasies cause you to expect more than the stock market can reasonably return for the risk you're willing to take.

An explanation of how the stock markets work will be useful to any investor, from novice to reasonably experienced, if it starts by offering guidance about how to approach investing and then gives you the basics you need to know. Now that you've considered the six points covered in this chapter, perhaps putting some of your thoughts in writing, you're now ready to start your journey into the stock market. If bonds interest you, start with that chapter. If funds are what you want to know more about, then proceed to that chapter. The key is to use this book as the foundation upon which you will build your understanding of the ever-changing investment markets and products, and how they may be useful to you as one of the vehicles you use on the road to attaining your financial goals.

Questions about taxation will inevitably come to mind as you read about dividends, interest payments and capital gains. Not only are some of the rules complicated and subject to change, but the specific calculation can depend on the person's taxable income and other individual factors. It is each person's responsibility to ensure that the amount of taxes is reported correctly to Her Majesty's Revenue and Customs within the stipulated time limits. For detailed, up-to-date explanations and examples of the current laws regarding the taxation the various types of investment income, talk to your stockbroker, financial adviser, accountant, or a tax professional. You will also find, clear and useful information at the government's website: www.direct.gov.uk.

2

THE TRADING MARKETS

The overall stock market (*not* the stock exchange) consists of two distinct parts: the primary market and the secondary market. The primary market is the part in which a company or other business enterprise issues securities (predominately shares and bonds) to investors in order to raise capital. The most common transactions in this segment of the market are initial public offerings (IPOs) and rights issues. When a company does an IPO, it issues securities for the first time to the public. Before that it has been essentially a private company. When a company does a rights issue, it offers more of the same shares directly to existing shareholders. Importantly, no trading occurs in the primary market. The transaction involves investing money in the company, either through its investment bankers in an IPO or directly with a rights issue. In exchange, investors receive shares or bonds.

Once a company or enterprise has issued stocks or bonds to institutions or the public, those securities can then be traded – that is, bought and sold – in the secondary market. The terms *trading market* and *secondary market* are synonyms. The London Stock Exchange is the best known and largest secondary market for securities in the United Kingdom. (It is no longer the only one, as you will discover later in this chapter. Today, there are several secondary or trading markets in the UK.) To make this trading possible, the enterprise issuing the securities applies simultaneously during the initial public offering process to two organisations: 1) the UK Listing Authority (UKLA); and 2) the London Stock Exchange (LSE), if the securities are going to trade there. Other exchanges have a similar admissions process.

The UKLA approves the company's prospectus and maintains the Official List – a list of those companies that meet its 'listing' rules and then qualify to trade on appropriate markets. From an investor's standpoint, one of the key roles of the UKLA is to make sure that each company provides an appropriate amount of information about itself so that potential investors can make an informed decision about the merits and risks of investing in the company or enterprise (especially the public).

For companies that want admission to trade on the London Stock Exchange's Main Market, there are two choices: Premium and Standard. The Standard Listing meets the minimum European Union (EU) qualifications and UK corporate governance code. The Premium option is significantly more stringent than Standard Listing. Companies that elect the Premium option *may* have their shares included in one of the Financial Times Stock Exchange (FTSE) indices. The third option is AIM which is usually the choice of younger, smaller companies for whom the cost of listing on the Main Market would be prohibitive. [Note: techMARK is not a listing option. Instead it allows similar companies (for example those in technology, healthcare, or medical sciences) across all three options to be monitored as a group.]

When a company applies to the London Stock Exchange seeking admission to trade on either the Main Market or AIM, the exchange makes sure the company meets the necessary requirements so that its securities will trade on the appropriate market of the exchange. Once admitted, the shares or bonds can begin trading in the secondary market – that is, on a stock exchange. While a young company may only qualify for AIM when it first goes public, its shares do not have to trade there forever. It is the goal of the many such companies to grow and qualify to trade in the Main Market. Such transfers are announced and praised.

Traditionally, a share or bond traded exclusively on one large national stock exchange – the one on which it was admitted for trading when the company went public. In essence, each national exchange had a monopoly business in the trading of a specific company's securities. Those days are gone and so are most of the traditional trading floors. Face-to-face negotiation between traders in a crowd is rare. Even if an exchange has a floor, like the NYSE Euronext, the vast majority of all trading is done on fully electronic trading platforms or facilities authorised in the UK by the Financial Services Authority, the FSA. In some markets, like AIM in London and the OTC Pink Market in the US, negotiations about price, quantity and trade execution can be done on the telephone; no central trading floor is needed. Additionally, some of the new electronic platforms facilitate the trading stock and bonds away from the London Stock Exchange as well as away from other national exchanges both within the UK and across borders in Europe. Many of the new computerised markets also trade many of the largest US-listed companies away from the NYSE-

Euronext and Nasdaq, the two largest New York-based exchanges where securities are traded in the US. The execution of buy and sell order for stocks or bonds away from the market to which they've been admitted for trading – i.e. listed – is known as *unlisted trading privileges* (UTP). The computerised platform that facilitates trading of a company's shares and bonds across country borders in Europe is called a *multilateral trading facility* (MTF). Some of the FSA-authorised MTFs or trading platforms on which LSE-listed stock can also trade include: BATS-ChiX, Burgundy (a specialist Scandinavian MTF), Equiduct, PLUS Markets (former OFEX), POSIT, and Turquoise. These are trading platforms in the secondary market that compete with the LSE. Additionally, there are about a half-dozen broker owned- and operated-MTFs, but they are not as independent.

What does the existence of these multiple trading markets mean to an individual investor – like you and me? It means two things. First, you have easier access to trade shares of companies beyond those that are listed and traded on the London Stock Exchange. Remember that other markets, especially the newer, fully electronic platforms, offer the ability to trade securities that are listed on other markets, like the NYSE Euronext or Nasdaq, for example. These securities do not trade on the LSE. And second, the more competition among the various trading venues results in better execution price for you the investor. While most people think their trades are routed to the 'floor' of the London Stock Exchange, it is not always the case. The most popular LSE-listed securities trade on multiple markets. Regulators view this development as creating more price competition and therefore better prices, as each market vies for the flow of orders. A customer's order can therefore be routed to any FSA-authorised market where the security trades. Each brokerage firm decides where to route the buy and sell orders it handles.

A brokerage firm tries to get the best price for its customer. This means executing an order to buy securities (stocks, bonds, ETFs, etc.) at the lowest price available at the time the order reaches the trading market, which in the old days would have been the trading floor. When a customer places an order to sell, the brokerage firm tries to execute the order at the highest price available at that time the order reaches the secondary market. Today at most firms, computers scan the different trading markets, including the London Stock Exchange, to find the best trading price. In fact, it is unlikely that a human being, other than your broker (if you use one) or yourself (if you do your own online trading), will be involved in the actual execution of your order, especially if it is for shares of large companies located in the UK, Europe, or the US.

The London Stock Exchange's Trading Systems

Today, secondary trading markets are increasingly computerised order-matching systems. This automated process is simple and, perhaps most important, fast. The amount of time from entering a buy or sell order until it is executed is referred to as *latency*. Low latency (the fastest execution time possible) is an important and highly publicised benefit in today's markets, especially for institutional investors. Computerised trades can be executed in microseconds.

Some markets – the London Stock Exchange is an example – maintain both a computerised order-execution system and a trading system that involves real people – called market makers – who bid to buy shares into their inventory and offer to sell shares out of their inventory throughout the trading session. The bid price and offer price for a particular security is referred to as a two-sided quote. As part of the quote the market maker also specifies the quantity of the security (the number of ordinary shares, for example) he or she is willing to buy at the bid price and sell at the offer price. The specified quantities are referred to as the 'size of the quote'.

The bid/offer quotes and quantities are published and disseminated via market data feeds in real time and delayed time (usually fifteen minutes) throughout the trading session. Users of this information – television stations, financial services companies, online trading sites, hedge funds (pooled investment vehicles for institutions and high net worth investors) and others – purchase two or more of these feeds. This is the source of the stock or bond prices as well as other information about the market that brokers quote to their customers.

At the LSE, two platforms had been used to trade shares of companies at different stages of their business development: the Stock Exchange Electronic Trading Service (SETS) and the Stock Exchange Automated Quotation system (SEAQ). The LSE has moved largely to SETS as its secondary market trading platform, although some stocks are still traded exclusively on SEAQ. SETS is an electronic book in which each security listed and traded on the LSE has its own page displaying all of the orders waiting to be executed in that security. These would be orders placed at, above, and below the current trading price. Using SETS buyers of a particular security can find sellers, and sellers can find buyers. Virtually all of the orders are matched or executed electronically via SETS.

The Two-Sided Quote

Because reports, especially financial television programmes, about trading in a particular company's shares cite the last price at which a trade occurred, many people think there is one price at which a stock or bond is bought or sold. This perception is incorrect. All securities have two prices: a *bid price* and an *offer price*. Together they are known as a two-sided quote. (Most people are aware of two-sided quotes in foreign exchange trans- actions, where there is a price at which the dealing company will buy the foreign currency from you and a higher price at which they will sell it to you.) Additionally the price quote for a security contains the quantities that can be bought at the offer price and sold at the bid price.

Bid	Offer
900/450p	457p/700

In the example above, the stock quote shows that someone (a market maker or another investor) is willing to buy 900 shares at 450p and someone is willing to sell 700 shares at 457p. The two-sided quote can be from one market maker. However, this is not always the case. The 900 shares on the bid side could be from one market maker or the aggregated number from several small orders, while the 700 shares on the offer side could be from a totally different market maker or group of orders. The quote for each security disseminated by most market data feeds is the best bid and offer (BBO) from among all market makers and trading markets where the security is traded. More specifically, the BBO in a two-sided quote is the *highest bid price* at which a customer's sell order will be executed and the *lowest offer price* at which a customer's buy order will be executed at that moment.

Using the example of the stock quote on the previous page, an investor's order to sell securities, provided the order is for no more than 900 shares, would be executed at £4.50, the bid price of the two-sided quote. An investor's buy order, provided the order is for no more than 700 shares, would be executed at £4.57, the offer price of a two-sided quote. The difference between these prices is widely known around the world as the *spread*. However, in the UK the difference between the best bid and lowest (or cheapest) offer is called the *touch*. It represents the profit potentially available for the market maker who buys that security into and sells it out of its own inventory at the currently displayed quote. Throughout a trading session, the bid/offer quote, its size (the number of shares at the bid and offer prices respectively) and the spread (or touch) will change frequently, especially during particularly active or volatile periods.

It's important to pay attention to the spread because it is the hidden cost of buying and selling any security. If you've ever bought a foreign currency and then sold

it back shortly afterwards, you were probably surprised
– even shocked – by the difference between the rates
you got on the two transactions. That difference is the
equivalent of the spread in the securities markets. Clearly
the wider the spread, the more the market price of the
stock or bond has to move before you can break even
and make a profit when you sell the security. In recent
years, the spread (or touch) on the biggest stocks with
the highest trading volume, such as Vodafone for
example, have narrowed to less than one 1p. (See Figure
2-1.) However, the spread on bid-offer price quotes for
mid-size and smaller companies can be much wider due
to the low trading volume.

Figure 2-1: Screenshot of a SETS Order Book Page for Vodafone
The long vertical line in the middle of the lower half of the Order Book page
divides the bid prices and related information (on the left side) from the offer

prices and related information (on the right side). The highlighted bar or area in the middle of the screen (it is yellow on the actual terminal) shows the best market – the highest bid price (178.25p) and the lowest offer price (178.35p) – at the time the shot was taken. The size of the quote (i.e. the number of shares available at those prices) is 54,411 shares at the bid price and 80,988 at the offer price. The numbers 8 on the bid side and 15 on the offer side of the highlighted bar indicate the number of individual orders that contain the total number of shares. If you add up the number of shares on all the orders standing on the bid side of the Order Book page at 178.25p, the total will be 54,411. The touch or spread is a 0.10p or a 10th of a penny. Other information displayed on the page includes the last sale price, the cumulative trading volume that day, the day's high and low prices, the 52-week high and low prices, the securities identification number, the dividend, and more.

The Basic Order Types

There are a surprisingly large number of different types of buy and sell orders used in the stock market, mostly by institutional and professional traders, to get a trade executed in a specific way. In fact many of the professionals now use complex mathematical formulas, called algorithms, to assist in the execution of the orders. However, typical retail investors (you and me) will find that five basic order types will serve most of their investment needs: a *market order*, a *limit order*, a *marketable limit order*, a *stop order*, and a *stop-limit order*. It is important to understand how each order works, the market expectation (or outlook) associated with it and the possible result associated with using each.

One basic feature of orders must be clearly understood first. When an order ticket is marked it can be marked one of four ways:

- **Buy**

  'Buy' means the investor is acquiring a securities position with the expectation that the price will rise over time. The words *buy* and *long* are synonyms in the investment markets.

- **Sell long**

  Order tickets are not simply marked 'sell'. Each ticket must specify whether it is an order to 'sell long' or 'sell short'. [Note: Most electronic order tickets that use 'sell' are programmed to mean 'sell long'.] 'Sell long' means an investor is selling securities that he or she already owns. Stated another way, the person is liquidating or closing out a long position in a security.

- **Sell short**

  'Sell short' is more complicated. It means that the investor is selling securities that he or she does not own. In fact, the securities being sold short have been borrowed on the investor's behalf by his or her brokerage firm. The investor is expecting the market price of the securities to decline over the short term (the time frame depends on your expectations) so they can buy them back at a lower price. The difference between the higher price at which the securities are initially sold short and the lower price at which they are eventually bought back is the profit to the investor. If, however, the market value of the security rises, the investor would realise a loss when he or she bought back the shares at a higher price than that at which they were sold short. Selling short involves unlimited loss because, in theory, the price of a security could rise by an unlimited amount before you're able to buy it back. [Note: Selling short cannot be done in the cash market in the UK. If you want to do so, you must use either the CFD (Contract for Difference) or Spreadbetting markets that facilitate trading on margin – i.e. making a partial payment on the full value of the position being established. Trading on margin increases risk and during adverse market moves, the broking firm can demand that you put up additional money (referred to as a margin call). Such complicated strategies involving leverage are beyond the scope of this book. However there are many websites that provide good information on these strategies and their risks.]

- **Buy to cover**
  'Buy to cover' means the investor is liquidating a short position. In reality, when the brokerage firm gets this order, it buys back the securities that were sold short for the investor. Remember, the brokerage firm had borrowed the securities for the customer. Now it returns those shares or bonds to the lender, which is usually another brokerage firm. Thus, the short position is covered or liquidated.

So as you learn about the five basic order types below, keep in mind that you can, for example, have 1) a market order to buy shares (i.e. go long); 2) a market order to sell long shares that you own (i.e. liquidate a position); 3) a market order to sell short shares (i.e. establish a short position); or 4) a market order to buy to cover a short position (i.e. cover a short sale). Your specific buy or sell instruction depends on whether you want to establish or liquidate a position, and on your expectation about the future price movement – rising or declining – of a specific security or the overall market.

Market Order

A market order, whether placed with a broker or using an electronic order ticket, contains only the name of the security and the amount in pounds (£). It does not specify a price or time, as the examples below illustrate:

buy £1,000 of BT
– or –
sell £1,000 of Vodafone

While I've used the words 'buy' and 'sell' above, because they are the verbs that most people would associate with an order, the specific terms in the UK are different. The market order above would be placed using the following wording:

Invest £1,000 in BT
– or –
Raise £1,000 from Vodafone

This wording is used to avoid confusion between the amount of money being invested or raised and the quantity of shares being bought or sold. It's an easy mistake to make when a customer places a verbal order.

A market order must be executed immediately at the BBO – the best bid price or offer price – available in the market at that time. Remember, an investor's market buy order will be executed at the lowest or cheapest offer price, while an investor's market sell order will be executed at the highest bid price. When placing a market order, a customer wants to buy into or sell out of a particular position now, not later. If the market price of the security changes by the time the order reaches the trading floor or the electronic trading platform where it will be executed, then the investor will get that current price. Again, a price and time are not specified on a market order.

Limit Order

When placing a limit order, the investor specifies the price at which he or she wants to buy or sell a specific security. For example:

sell £1,000 of Burberry Group at 1,260p
– or –
buy £1,000 of Morgan Sindall at 700p

Importantly, when a limit order is placed, it is understood that the order will be executed only at the specified price *or better*. What does 'or better' mean? Using the examples above, the investor who places the sell limit order on Burberry Group shares wants to sell them at 1,260p *or higher*. The investor placing the buy limit order on Morgan Sindall wants to buy the shares at 700p *or lower*.

A sell limit order can be used in two scenarios. In the first, the investor owns Burberry Group shares. The shares are currently trading at 1,220p. She believes they are about to reach a peak price around 1,260p. She wants to sell long (liquidate) the shares at the peak price or higher, before an anticipated decline perhaps caused by profit-taking by other investors. So she places a sell limit order at 1,260p, which is *above the current market price of the stock*. If the market price of Burberry reaches 1,260p or higher the investor's sell order will be executed. If, however, the shares never reach 1,260p or begin to decline in value before reaching the limit price, then the investor's shares will never be sold. She could end up still owning the shares as the price declines.

In the second scenario, the customer does not own Burberry shares. However, he believes that the shares are nearing a peak price and will decline sharply. He uses the limit order to sell short the shares at 1,260 or higher, in anticipation of a price decline that will enable him to buy back the shares at a lower price and therefore make a profit on the transaction. If the market never reaches 1,260p then the short position won't be established. The risk that the short seller faces is that the price of the stock rises to 1,260p limit price, the short sale order is executed, and then, instead of declining, the price continues to rise. The investor would then have to pay more in order to buy back the securities than he received when he sold them short. The result would be a loss.

A buy limit order is typically used to buy securities on a dip in price, before an anticipated rally. Using the Morgan Sindall example, let's say the market price for the shares has dropped from 1,100p and the shares are currently trading at 770p. Based on your research, you believe the stock will eventually drop to 700p. For you, this would be an attractive price at which to buy the stock. You also think other investors will begin buying the stock at this point and subsequently the price will rise. So with the shares currently trading at 770p, you place your limit order at 700p – *below the share's current market value*. If Morgan Sindall drops to the limit price, the order would only be executed at 700p or lower, and hopefully the share price will rise. If, however, it continues to decline instead of rising, then the investor would be losing money on the shares he just bought. If the stock begins to rally before the price reaches 700p, then the buy limit order will not be executed and the customer would miss the rally in the stock's price.

A buy limit order can be used to cover or buy back shares that have been sold short. Let's imagine the investor sold short Morgan Sindall when the price was at 1,300p. The price has declined to 750p. The investor believes that the share price will continue to drop to 700p or slightly lower before it begins to rally. The investor places a buy limit order at 700p. If the shares trade at 700p the order will be executed and the short position liquidated. If, however, the shares begin to rally before reaching 700p, the buy limit order will not be executed and the customer will begin losing some of the profits made on the short position.

Here is a quick, easy-to-understand summary of the placement and use of the two limit order examples.

- A buy limit order is placed below the current market price of a security and is used to buy into the market on a dip in price, before an expected rise.
- A sell limit order is placed above the current market price of a security and is used to sell out of a position (or sell short) at a peak in a share's price movement, before an expected decline.

Because limit orders are placed 'away from' – i.e. above or below – a security's current market price, they are held on a central electronic order book (called a *central limit order book*) at the price point specified. The order remains there during the trading session, until the security's price reaches or passes through the specified price, and then the limit order is automatically executed.

Marketable Limit Order

This is a variation on the limit order that is used on many of the computerised order-matching systems. Unlike a traditional limit order, which is entered below or above the market, a marketable limit order is entered *at* the current price level at which a share is trading. In placing this order, the customer is making sure that the order will be executed only at the current price level *or better*.

If, for example, a share is trading at 770p and you want to buy shares at this price only, you would enter a marketable limit order with a specified price of 770p. Your order would be eligible for immediate execution. The advantage of a marketable limit order is that if the share price unexpectedly moved higher than 770p, then your order would not be executed. If the share price moved lower than 770p, the order would be executed because the lower price would be better than your specified limit price.

Two logical questions should immediately come to mind: why wouldn't the investor simply enter a market order? Wouldn't it be executed at 770p, the current market price? The answer to this second question is 'it might be'. If you entered a market order, which specifies no price, and the share's price moved sharply up or down as your order was being routed for execution, the order might be executed at or near 770p, but it could also be executed significantly above or below 770p.

Similarly, a marketable limit order to sell would specify a price at the current market and therefore would be eligible for execution at the current market price or higher. Therefore, a marketable limit order gives an investor the certainty that the order will be executed at the current market price or better, but never worse.

Professional traders use a marketable limit order in a more aggressive way. They will often enter a marketable limit order at a price that is 'better' than the current market. Their goal is to take advantage of the liquidity that's in the market at various price points on the central order book.

If, for example, a share is currently trading at 770p, a trader might enter a marketable limit order to buy at 772p. With the share's market price already below – i.e. better than – the marketable limit order's specified price, the order would begin being executed immediately at 770p, then 771p, and would continue as the price reaches 772p. Once the price goes above 772p, the execution would stop if the entire order has not already been executed.

Now let's look at this from the point of view of a trader who wants to sell. Let's say the share is currently trading at 1,260p. The trader enters a marketable limit order to sell at 1,257p. The current market price is already *better* (higher) than the specified sell limit price, so the security would start to be sold at 1,260, then 1,259p, then 1,258p, and then 1,257p. If the entire order is not executed by the time the share price falls below 1,257p, then the execution would stop.

Professional traders use marketable limit orders in this way when they have a large buy or sell order to execute and want to 'sweep the book' – i.e. immediately grab all of the liquidity (the quantity of shares) that is available to be bought or sold between their marketable limit order price and the security's current market price.

In summary, a marketable limit order is always placed at or slightly better than a security's current market price so that it's eligible for immediate execution, but only at the specified price or better.

- A marketable limit order to buy is placed at or slightly above a security's current market price.
- A marketable limit order to sell is placed at or slightly below a security's current market price.

Stop Order (aka Stop-Loss Order)

Like a limit order, the investor must specify a price, called the stop price, when the order is placed. However, with a stop order, when the security's price hits the specified price, the order is transformed into a market order, and is executed at the security's current BBO, whatever that may be. This is the most useful order for investors who want to limit losses or protect profits. The following example illustrates how this order is commonly – and wisely – used.

This first example shows how an investor can effectively use a sell stop order. Let's say you've just bought a company's shares, which are trading at 770p. When you buy these shares you are, of course, concerned that the price may decline suddenly and precipitously, resulting in a significant loss on the position. To protect yourself (that is, limit your potential loss), you place a sell stop order at 750p, *below the price at which you bought the stock*. It's important to understand that the price you specify on a sell stop order is only a trigger. If the share price suddenly plummets and hits your 750p price, the stop order is immediately transformed into a market order. Subsequently, it is executed at whatever the market price may be at that moment – which may be at, above or below your stop price. In this case, the sell stop order would limit your loss on the position to around 20p; but the loss could be greater if the stock is tanking or in a free fall as a result of an unexpected negative announcement. Don't forget you can only sell the shares if a buyer is willing to pay for them. Negative news would mean buyers would only want to pay lower prices for the stock, therefore your losses would increase.

As the price of a security you own rises, producing a gain, you will want to protect that gain against an unexpected drop in the market, beyond a security's normal volatility. Placing a sell stop order below a long position so that you protect part of the gains you've made is a prudent strategy. And if the stock continues to move up, adjust the specified price on your sell stop order accordingly. This strategy is often referred to as a trailing stop-loss order.

The scenarios discussed in these two examples illustrate two important features of a stop order. First, a sell stop order is placed below the market when it's being used to limit the losses or protect the profits on a long position – i.e. securities that you own. And second, when the market hits or passes through your stop price, you are guaranteed that your order will be executed (because it becomes a market order), but you have no idea what price you will get. Your hope is that the price will be at or very near the order's stop price.

How far below a security's current market price do you set the stop price? That depends upon your (or your broker's) analysis of the share's volatility. You don't want to set the price too close so that the share's normal volatility causes the stop order to be triggered and executed. The practical way of determining the price you want to specify on a sell stop order is to set it based on the amount you're willing to lose on the position or the amount of the gain you want to protect if the security has risen in value.

The following scenarios illustrate how a buy stop order is typically used. It is used to limit losses or protect the profits when you sell short a security. Remember that the risk of selling short is that the price of the security rises. If that happens then the investor must buy back the security at a higher price than the price at which it was sold short, thereby losing money. If, for example, an investor believes that the market price of a company's shares is about to decline, he may sell short the security at 950p. To limit the potential loss in case the security rallies unexpectedly, the investor would enter a buy stop order at 980p – *above the security's current market price*. If the worst-case scenario occurs, the buy stop order would be triggered and transformed into a market order when the share price reaches 980p. It would then be eligible for immediate execution at whatever the market price might be at that moment. The purchase of the security would cover the investor's short position. [Remember: a stop order is guaranteed to be executed if the stock hits or passes through your specified stop price, but you have no idea what the actual execution price will be.]

Once a short position has been established and becomes profitable (as a result of a price decline), a prudent investor may want to place a buy stop order just above the security's current market price to protect the gains made, just in case there's an unexpected rally in the market. If the market price of the short security continues to move lower, producing more profits, the investor can lower the specified price on the buy stop order accordingly. In this case the investor is using a trailing stop loss order (specifically a buy stop) to protect the profits made on a short position.

So, to effectively use a stop order for its stop-loss feature, it should be placed as follows:

- A sell stop order is placed below the current market price of securities that you own in order to protect against an unexpected price decline.
- A buy stop order is placed above the current market value of a short position in order to protect it from an unexpected price rise.

Stop-Limit Order

When an investor places a stop-limit order, he or she must specify both a stop price and a limit price. For example:

sell £1,000 of Burberry Group at 1,260p Stop 1,250 Limit
– or –
buy £1,000 of Morgan Sindall at 700p Stop 710 Limit

On a sell stop-limit order, the limit price is the same or lower than the stop price; and on a buy stop-limit order the limit price will be the same or higher than the stop price.

Think of a stop-limit order as a more cautious version of a stop order. Remember that with a stop order, your order is transformed into a market order when the shares trade at or pass through your stop price. Your order is then executed at the best bid or offer price available at that time. You have no idea what price you will get. With a stop-limit, however, there is an important difference. When the security's market value trades at or passes through the specified stop price, your order is transformed into a limit order, *not* a market order. The limit order is then executed only at your specified price or better.

So translating the intent of this order into everyday language, the customer who places the sell-limit order for Burberry Group wants to begin selling the shares when the market price hits 1,260p (the stop price), but doesn't sell it for less than 1,250p (the limit price). With the buy stop-limit order the customer is directing the trader to begin buying the stock when the shares hit the stop price of 700p, but not to pay more than 710p. In both of these cases the investor has the same bullish or bearish outlook as a person who places a stop order; however if he or she cannot establish or liquidate the position at a certain price (the specified limit price), then the person would rather not sell the position or buy into the market respectively.

Stop-limit orders are used effectively when they are placed away from the current market in the following ways:

- A sell stop-limit order is placed below the current market price of securities that you own, but you don't want to sell below your limit price.
- A buy stop-limit order is placed above the current market value enabling you to buy into a rally, but you only want to buy up to your specified limit price and no higher.

The chart opposite shows how the buy and sell versions of five types of orders are placed relative to the prevailing market price of a security.

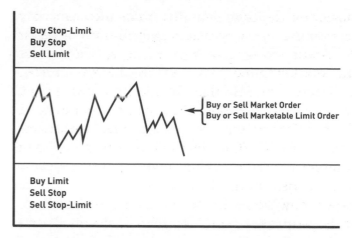

Figure 2.2: Placement of orders
Market orders and marketable limit orders are placed at the current market for immediate execution. Limit, stop and stop-limit orders are placed 'away from' the current market (above or below as shown). Their execution is contingent upon the market reaching the price specified on the order when it is entered. If the market never reaches the specified price then a limit, stop or stop-limit order will not be executed. A recent upgrade to the SETS order book featured in Figure 2-1 is the ability to leave stop-loss and stop-limit orders at specific prices on the book. In Figure 2-1, the orders standing below and above the highlighted Best Bid and Offer are most likely buy limit (below) and sell limit (above) orders.

How long can these orders stand in the market? Keep in mind that market and marketable limit orders must be executed or filled immediately. However, orders that are placed 'away from' (above or below) the current market price have a time limit, unless certain notations are included when the order is placed. If no time limit is specified, then the duration of a limit, stop or stop-limit order is a day. If the market does not move to a price where the order can be filled, then the order is cancelled. If there has been a partial execution of the order, then the remaining unexecuted portion will be cancelled.

If you want your order to stand in the market beyond a day, then you must specify GTC, which means 'good till cancelled'. In this case, the order could in theory stand in the market indefinitely. However, brokerage firms set limits requiring, for example, that an order with a GTC notation must be renewed at the end of every month. If you fail to do so, then the order is automatically cancelled.

Understanding the order types is key to understanding what causes the price of a security to fluctuate throughout the day. At various times during a stock exchange's trading session, there may be more people buying stocks and shares in response to various research or news reports, so the price will rise. At other times there may be more people selling shares (selling long or selling short) and this will cause the price of the security to decline. As each of the different investor's orders is executed, eventually all of the shares being bid or offered at the given prices of a two-sided quote will be exhausted. This means there will be no shares available at that price. When that occurs, the price of the security moves to the next best bid or offer price where orders are standing on the central limit order book, which holds all orders placed below and above the market until they are executed.

Another factor that affects a security's volatility is the amount of the security available to be bought or sold at a given bid or offer price. When explaining the two-sided quote earlier, I referred to the amount available as the size of the quote. This is also referred to as the *depth of the market*. The greater the depth at a specific price, the more trades are required to exhaust the number of shares available and thus cause the price to move. Hence, greater depth is associated with lower volatility and easier order execution.

Additionally, there are firms, called market makers, who are also bidding to buy stock into their inventory and offering to sell stock out of their inventory. There may be multiple market makers in the same security competing for the flow of orders coming to the market to be executed. The greater the number of participants – individuals, institutions, brokerage firms and market makers – who want to trade a given security, the easier it is for all investors to buy and sell. This is called a *liquid market*. It is characterised by quick executions, lower volatility, and smaller bid–offer spreads. In contrast, a market with few buyers or sellers is described as an *illiquid market*. It is characterised by longer order execution times, greater volatility, and wider bid–offer spreads. In short, the cost of trading increases.

The Cost of Trading

There are two significant costs involved in trading security. One is the spread or touch that was discussed earlier in the section on Two-Sided Quotes on page 23. The second cost is the commission. Stockbrokers act as agents in the transaction, bringing a buyer and seller together. For this service, they charge a commission. The amount of commission is typically *the greater of* a minimum fixed amount or a fixed percentage of the total cost of the trade. Execution-only brokers typically charge the smallest commission.

This fee is usually charged when an order is executed, not when an order is placed. To execute your first trade will generally require cash up front – i.e. the money must already be in your account – for at least the total amount of the trade. The firm does this in order to protect itself. The specific terms and fees will vary depending on the type of account you've opened at that particular advisory or execution-only firm. Regardless of the type of broking firm being used, cash must be in an Individual Savings Account (ISA) or Self-Invested Personal Pension (SIPP) before a purchase transaction can be entered and executed.

The other cost that a customer pays when buying (not selling) shares is stamp duty. It is a small, fixed percentage of the trade and is set by Her Majesty's Revenue and Customs (HMRC). It is currently levied at a rate of 0.5% on the total purchase price of equities, including the commission if the firm executing the trade sold you shares out of its own inventory. Stamp duty, however, is not levied on the purchase price of bonds.

Summary

The day-to-day price movement of a specific security and of the overall market is driven by the buy and sell orders that flow into the market and are executed. As all of the shares being bid or offered at a specific price are exhausted, the price moves on to the next point where orders that have been placed either below or above the market (and are held on the electronic central order book as shown in Figure 2-1) are now ready to be executed, or it moves to quotes disseminated by market makers, indicating the prices at which they are willing to buy the security into and sell securities out of their own inventory.

Low-latency (aka high-speed) computerised trading, combined with order-matching systems, has brought about a significant change in the types of orders that are used, especially among industry professionals. While the public is still likely to use market orders to buy and sell securities because they want immediate execution, professional traders, with their high-speed order-routing and execution systems, increasingly use marketable limit orders to establish and liquidate positions. At high-frequency trading firms, people are often not involved in the trading. Computers, using proprietary algorithms, can establish long or short positions using various order types and then realise profits (or limit losses) without a trader's active participation.

Today the traders may be housed in a specific building, but the trading will take place on computer servers and at the trading desks of market makers. The objective, however, is the same as it has always been: to get the customer's buy or sell order executed at the best available price, or one that is fair and reasonable given the market conditions at that time.

As an investor you must always be aware of the cost of investing – especially the spread. If an execution-only broking firm does not display *both* the bid and the offer prices for a specific security, in effect hiding its spread or touch, then it is probably unwise to use that firm. If the spread is more than 1%, which is likely to be the case with some mid-size and smaller company stocks that do not trade frequently, then you might want to use a full-service broking firm that will negotiate a better price (thus narrowing the spread) or offer advice on how to place the different order types to get a better price. These last two services are standard at a full-service broking firm and will obviously cost you more commission. However, if you regularly buy and sell securities that have wide spreads, you may find that the cost of having your trades executed at better prices equals or is less than the charges at an execution-only firm, and you have the option of getting advice from a broker whenever you want it.

Post-Trade Clearing and Settlement

After a trade is executed, it must go through the clearing and settlement process. Clearing is the process of making sure both parties (called counterparties) involved in the execution of the trade agree to all of its details, commonly referred to as the *trade data*. These include the specific security, the execution price, the quantity of the trade, the date and time the trade was executed, the specific market in which it was executed, and the broking firms (or the firms representing them) involved in the trade, and other related information. Today, most orders are executed through automated systems that capture both the buy side trade data and the sell side trade data. This is referred to as a *locked-in trade*, and all of the data on both sides should match up perfectly. At those times when the trade has been executed manually and for some reason the trade data does not match, then the broking firms must resolve the difference or bust the trade (i.e. undo it).

Once the trade has been cleared, it is then ready to be settled. Settlement is the orderly exchange of cash and securities on a given date. The number of days from trade date (represented by the letter T) to the settlement date differs with the type of security. The standard settlement dates are set by the FSA. Equities settle three business days after the trade date. This is referred to as a T+3 settlement. Corporate bonds also settle in T+3. Gilts, however, settle in T+1, the next business day after the trade. [Note: There are some exceptions for equities where broking firms can permit settlement in T+10, even up to T+15. Such non-standard settlements cost more.]

The time in between the trade date and settlement date is when clearing occurs. The counterparties do not have to send or receive securities and money among themselves. Instead, this procedure is centralised at a clearing house. In the UK, trades in securities are cleared and settled between the counterparties through LCH. Clearnet. (In the US, it is the Depository Trust and Clearing Corporation or DTCC.) It acts as a third party, inserting itself between clearing firms representing the counterparties of the trade. This means that the counterparties deliver their positions to, or receive their position from the clearing house. This central position gives the clearing house an accurate picture of potential problems and risks in the market so that it can take the necessary steps to manage that risk. This usually involves requesting a clearing member to deposit additional cash or other collateral in their account at the clearing house.

At the end of each business day, a clearing house makes sure that the correct number of securities positions and the associated debit or credit of cash are assigned to the correct clearing broking firm. It's important to know that not all broking firms are members of a clearing house. Firms that do not want to bear the significant financial responsibility and cost associated with being such a member establish an agreement with a clearing firm that, in turn, handles the process on behalf of the non-clearing member.

Increasingly, one of the less-talked-about roles in securities markets is to 'dematerialise' securities. In short, paper or physical certificates are gradually but surely disappearing. More and more securities are held in *book-entry form* in which there is only an electronic record of ownership. A customer's trade confirmation (called a *contract note*) that contains all of the details of the trade (i.e. name of the security bought or sold, the quantity, the execution price, commissions, the trade date, the settlement date, etc.) serves as proof of ownership. The securities purchased, instead of being held in the customer's name, are held in a nominee account. This means that the securities are pooled together on the register in the name of the broker's nominee company or in the clearing house's nominee company. A nominee company is one that is not permitted, by its Articles of Association, to trade. Its sole role is to act as a company into whose name investments can be registered. More specifically, stock registered into a broker's nominee is usually pooled into a single holding for each company in which clients of the firm have an investment. The 'break out', which represents the records of the underlying holdings for each individual client, is held by the broking firm. The best firms make sure that its records of ownership are current and accurate by reconciling them daily through Crest.

Holding securities on a nominee basis has several advantages and some disadvantages. The three key advantages are: 1) it is less costly because no certificate has to be printed; 2) it is safer because the customer has no certificate that can be lost, stolen, or mutilated, and 3) it makes selling the securities much easier. Since the nominee company is under the control of the brokerage firm, it means that a customer does not have to deliver the actual certificates to effect a sale.

The disadvantages are the added cost as well as no access to annual reports and other information. Some firms charge for holding securities in a nominee account and some do not. Those in this second group will usually have an inactivity fee that is levied if the client does not trade in the account for three months, for example. Because the securities are pooled on the register in the name of the nominee company, the brokerage firm will be sent only one set of the company's annual reports, notices of AGMs, proxies and other documents. The firm would not have enough copies to send to shareholders even if it wanted to. Some firms use Broadridge (formerly ADP) to offer individual clients copies of the annual reports, documents, and voting proxies for the UK companies whose securities they own. Annual reports are available to investors online though.

Ultimately, securities will be dematerialised. In Germany and Japan, customers can no longer get paper certificates, and in the US it is increasingly difficult and expensive to do so. In the UK, it is still possible to obtain a stock or bond certificate at the time of purchase or to have the holding transferred from a brokerage firm's nominee company into your own name, at which time a certificate will be sent to you. This is not inexpensive. While holding a physical certificate may reinforce your sense of actually owning the security, it makes selling it more expensive. It also holds up the selling process because the certificate will generally have to be transferred into a brokerage firm's nominee account before the sale can take place. These added costs and delays are the reason why the industry wants all securities to be held electronically in book-entry form despite resistance from some people. Investors will therefore have to become as diligent about keeping track of their trade confirmations and account statements as they have been in the past about the safekeeping of paper certificates.

3

SHARES: ORDINARY AND PREFERENCE

When most people think about a stock exchange, they typically think about trading shares. In reality there are other types of securities that trade there, including bonds (corporate, sovereign, etc.) and *exchange-traded funds* (ETFs). However, it is stories of the wealth that can be made with shares that capture people's imaginations and make the stock market intriguing and enticing.

A share represents part ownership in a business and gives the shareholder the ability to participate in and profit from its growth. Shares are also referred to as *equity securities*, a term denoting a stake in the business. All shares have the right to receive *dividends*. These are a portion of the company's after-tax profits called *earnings*. Dividends, however, are not paid automatically; instead, they must be declared by a company's Board of Directors (BOD). The Board usually meets twice a year (or sometimes once a quarter) to determine the exact amount of the dividend and when it will be paid out. The amount and regularity of the dividend can depend on which of the two types of equity shares an investor owns: ordinary shares or preference shares.

Ordinary Shares

Called *common stock* in the US, *ordinary shares* are the type of equity security issued most frequently when a company does a floatation or initial public offering. Ordinary shares are part of every corporation's or limited company's capital structure. The quantity that is initially issued during an IPO depends on how much capital a company wishes to raise, the price per share its underwriter or investment banker believes investors will pay, and how much control the owners are willing to relinquish in exchange for the money.

The total number of shares that a company is authorised to issue (called authorised but unissued shares or authorised share capital) is specified in its Articles of Association. Unless the company's Articles of Association require a special or extraordinary resolution, a company can increase its authorised shares by passing an ordinary resolution. It must send a copy of the resolution and a notice of the increase in authorised shares to the governmental organisation, Companies House. Most companies issue only a small percentage of these as part of an IPO. Later on, the company may issue additional quantities of its authorised shares if it wants to raise more capital. When a company does this, the number of shares available to be traded on a stock exchange increases. This issuance of more of the same ordinary shares already trading on a stock exchange is referred to as a secondary offering.

Investors who own a company's ordinary shares have rights that are stated in the company's Articles of Association. These rights are:

Right to Vote

Ordinary shares are sometimes called *voting shares* because only they offer owners this right. (Preference shares, discussed later, do not.) Among the important issues ordinary shareholders can vote on are:

- Election of the Board of Directors;
- Changes in the Articles of Association;
- A merger acquisition, or occasionally a significant disposal;
- An increase in the Authorised Capital;
- Director's remuneration. [Note: This is being discussed.]

Voting takes place at the Annual General Meeting (AGM) and at an Extraordinary General Meeting (EGM), if one is held. If shareholders attend either of these meetings, they can vote themselves and sometimes ask the management questions. However, many people choose not to attend the AGM or EGM. Instead, they sign a *proxy* giving someone else (usually the chairman of the company, a specific Board member, or a large shareholder) the power to vote their shares.

In the UK, companies issue one class of ordinary shares. However, it is becoming increasingly common for companies, particularly in the US and Latin America, to issue two classes of ordinary shares with different voting rights. One class is issued to company insiders – the owners as well as any venture capitalists or large, rich investors who were involved in the early financing of the company. The other class is issued to the public – you and me. The first group typically has more than one vote per share, while the second group will have only one vote or a fractional vote per share.

This is referred to as *weighted voting rights*. It clearly enables the owners and senior managers to retain control of the company, while leaving regular shareholders with little say in how the company is managed, or regarding any changes in the Articles of Association in issuing different classes of ordinary shares. This practice is frowned upon in the UK.

Right to Receive Dividends

All dividends must be declared by a company's Board of Directors and are usually paid out twice a year, although some companies pay quarterly. The amount of the payment is totally at the Board's discretion. Generally, people think dividend payments depend on a company's profitability and should increase over time. Since the recession began in 2007–08, there are numerous examples of companies that reduced or totally stopped their dividend payments because of the decrease in their profits and earnings. Understandably, investors sold the shares and looked for companies that paid better, more reliable dividends.

In reality, profitability is only part of the Board's reason for declaring these payments to shareholders. Equally important is its attitude towards dividends. Some Boards believe in paying substantial dividends regularly and increasing the amount periodically. They do this because they want the company's shareholder base to know that the payments are dependable. The shareholders are probably people for whom these dividend payments are part of the income they live on. Pharmaceutical companies are an example of a business sector that typically pays regular and substantial dividends.

Other companies, Warren Buffett's Berkshire

Hathaway being a prime example, do not believe in paying dividends to ordinary shareholders regardless of how much profit the company makes. [Note: As a large holding company, Berkshire receives dividends from the companies in which it invests.] Buffett wants his investors to adhere to his 'buy and hold' philosophy. Therefore, the only way you will make any return on Berkshire stock is by purchasing it and holding it over the long-term.

Still other Boards choose to invest all of the company's earnings back into their business, paying nothing to shareholders. This is typical of growth companies. Many of them are very profitable, but use the money for further investment in research, new product development, marketing and acquiring new talent. Investors in these types of companies hope to make money from the capital growth of the share price, not from dividend payments.

In the past, companies gave shareholders the option to receive additional ordinary shares in the company instead of a cash dividend payment. This is known as a *scrip offering*. Fewer and fewer companies in the UK offer this service today because of small but quite inconvenient recordkeeping issues related to the small amounts of money and small numbers of shares involved.

Pre-Emptive Right
This is the right of each ordinary shareholder to maintain his or her proportionate ownership in the company. If, for example, you own 5% of a company's issued-and-outstanding shares and the company proposes issuing an additional 1,000,000 new shares, then you, the ordinary shareholder, have the right of first refusal to

buy 5% (50,000) of the 1,000,000 new shares. This right is implemented through a process called a *rights issue*. Basically, existing shareholders have the right to subscribe to their percentage of the new offering for a limited period of time, usually 30 or 60 days. During this period, current shareholders can purchase their portion of new shares at a subscription price, which is always lower than the shares' current market price.

The shareholder has a second option. He or she can sell the rights, just as he or she would an ordinary share, to someone who really wants to subscribe to the additional shares.

The shareholder's third option is to simply let the rights expire at the end of the designated period. If, however, an existing shareholder chooses not to subscribe to the additional shares, or lets his or her rights expire, then the company can offer the new shares to new investors. When this happens, an existing shareholder's percentage of ownership will decline. In the US, the pre-emptive right is often described as 'arcane' – old and out of date. Many US companies do not offer the pre-emptive right. However in Europe and Asia, rights issues occur more frequently.

Right to Participate in a Company's Capital Growth

The market price of ordinary shares rises and falls with the fortunes of the company that issued them. If the business becomes more profitable and its earnings increase, then the share price should rise. If the company does poorly, showing losses or a decline in turnover, its ordinary share prices will fall.

When the ordinary share price rises to a certain amount, the Board of Directors may decide to split the company's stock. Its objective is to make the ordinary shares more affordable to typical retail investors. This is a common practice in the US, where share prices are much higher than in the UK. The market price at which this decision is made is totally subjective; there is no consistency within or across business sectors.

When a stock split occurs, an investor owns more shares; however, the price is adjusted downward by the percentage of the stock split. As a result, the investor owns the same total value of stock before and after the split. For example, an investor owns 100 ordinary shares whose price is 1,640p (total value: £1,640) and the company announces a one-for-one stock split – i.e. one new share for each existing share held. (Interestingly, in the US, this would be called a two-for-one stock split.) After the split, the investor will own 200 shares with a market value of 820p [1,640p ÷ 2] per share and the total value of the investor's holding will still be £1,640. The investor now owns more shares, each of which can increase in price as the company fortunes improve, and will receive dividend payments on these, hopefully increasing over time.

In the US, the stock split described above is called a positive stock split because it results in the investors ending up with more shares. In the US there is another type of stock split that does not exist in the UK. It's called a *negative* or *reverse stock split*. It results in a reduction in the number of shares an investor owns. Let's say a person owns 1,000 ordinary shares with a current market price of 52p (total value: £520). The company announces a one-for-ten reverse stock split. This means that for every ten shares the investor currently owns, he or she will get one. After the split, the investor will own 100 shares with a market value of 520p per share (total value: still £520). A US company will choose to do a negative or reverse stock split when its price has dropped so low that the company risks being de-listed or downgraded from the US stock market (e.g. NYSE Euronext or Nasdaq) on which it currently trades.

Claims on the Company's Assets in a Liquidation

An ordinary shareholder has claims on a company's remaining assets should it go into liquidation. That's the good news. The bad news is that these investors are last in line behind all of types of securities issued by the company. The chance of getting back any of the money you invested in the shares of a company that becomes insolvent is zero. Losing all of the money invested in a company is the biggest risk an ordinary shareholder faces.

Classification of Ordinary Shares

Like many investment instruments, ordinary shares are described or categorised in different ways. This organisational methodology helps to differentiate among the characteristics of specific ordinary shares as well as the company that issued them. It also makes it easier to compare and contrast companies that are in the same or different groups. Ordinary shares are classified in newspapers, magazines and research reports, as well as by financial services firms and rating agencies, in four ways: 1) by business sector; 2) by the size or capitalisation of the company; 3) by the phase of the company's development; and 4) by the way the company and its shares react to economic changes.

Financial Times Share Service

Aerospace & Defence

Notes	Price	Wks% Chg	Div	Cov	Mcap £m	Last xd
AvonRub...	304	-5.0	3	8.4	93.4	10.8
RaF Sys	272.90	+6.7	18	1.9	8,847.2	19.10
Chemring .†	397	+1.8	12.40	3.9	766.8	13.7
Cobham...†	178.30	+7.1	6.17	2.2	1,923.1	12.10
Harnpson...	5.55	+16.8			15.5	9'10
Meggitt...†	384	+5.1	9.55	2.5	2,988.4	10.8
RollsRyc .◆	720.50	+6.3	14.85	6.2	13,489.5	10'10
Senior.....†	174.20	+7.5	3.27	4.1	700.7	26.10
UltraElc ...‡	£14.40	+2.3	35.70	3.0	992.6	17.8
UMECO....‡	364.50	+8.6	15.50	1.0	175.8	7.9

Automobiles & Parts

Notes	Price	Wks% Chg	Div	Cov	Mcap £m	Last xd
FordMtr $..◆	704.55	+11.9			26,773.6	7.06
GKN......†	193.70	+14.2	5.50	3.6	3,008.4	10.8
Torotrak....	32.25	+5.3			53.0	
ToyotaV...◆	£21.29	+5.5	¥50	0.2	73,761.3	28.9
Volkswgn C◆	£97.64	+12.8	€2.20	16.1	28,811.5	4.5

Banks

Notes	Price	Wks% Chg	Div	Cov	Mcap £m	Last xd
ANZ A$...	◆£13.61xd	+15.7	$2	1.0	35,853.9	10.11
BankAm $	◆367.31xd	+10.0	4c		37,730.4	30.11
BankIre€...	7.65	+14.4			2,304.9	5.08
BkNvaS C$.◆	£31.07	+4.8	$2.05	2.2	33,851.0	30.9
Barclays ..◆	190.65xd	+22.5	5.50	4.6	23,252.5	9.11
BcoSant ..†	495.75	+11.6	60c	1.4	42,472.1	1.8
CanImp C$|◆	£44.67	+5.9	$3.54	2.1	17,894.2	26.9
FirstRandℓ.	160.21	+9.3	81c	2.9	9,032.6	10.10
HSBC....◆|◆	510.70xd	+9.3	43.33c	2.0	91,251.0	23.11
LlydsBkg .◆	25.39	+9.5			17,449.7	8.08
RylBkC C$|◆	£30.40	+13.7	$2.08	1.9	43,720.3	24.10
RBS.......◆	21.63	+15.4			12,811.1	3.08
StandCh |◆	£14.53	+14.1	79.33c	2.5	34,589.2	10.8
7.375%Pf.	104.50		7.38		100.4	14.9
8.25%Pf ..	112.13		8.25		111.3	14.9
TntoDom C$|◆	£45.90	+8.9	$2.68	2.4	41,422.7	3.10
VTB Bank $.	291.35	+18.3	4.18c		15,738.6	28.4
Westpc A$ ◆	£14.06xd	+15.0	$2.23	1.0	42,604.9	7.11

ⓘ **Get annual reports at www.ft.com/ir**

Basic Resource (Ex Mining)

Notes	Price	Wks% Chg	Div	Cov	Mcap £m	Last xd
Ferrexpo ..	294.50	+14.4	6.60c	14.9	1,733.5	10.8
IntFerMet ..	20.25	+1.3			112.2	10.08
Mondi ....†	463.60	+11.7	27.50c	2.0	1,371.2	17.8
UPM-Kym€	739.58	+12.0	55c	1.7	3,882.6	8.4
Vale R$ ....◆	£15.14	+6.9	1.32		49,314.3	17.10

Chemicals

Notes	Price	Wks% Chg	Div	Cov	Mcap £m	Last xd
AZElecMat.	249	+8.9	4.22c	66.2	948.5	7.9
Bayer€....◆	£40.65	+9.1	€1.50	1.5	33,614.5	2.5

Financial General

Notes	Price	Wks% Chg	Div	Cov	Mcap £m	Last xd
3i.........†	190.30	+5.6	5.10		1,847.7	15.6
AberAsM †	203.40	+9.9	7.60	1.5	2,378.7	11.5
APR Engy..	978.25	+0.9			765.1	
Ashmore...	346.90	+11.7	14.50	1.9	2,453.9	2.11
BrewDlph..	127.80	+6.6	7.10	1.3	311.0	24.8
Camellia...	£95.50	+0.5	110	12.3	265.4	5.10
CharlsSt...†	265xd	+1.0	11	1.7	119.9	23.11
CharlsTy ..†	126.25	+0.6	7.71	1.7	50.9	5.10
CityLonGp †	61.50	-3.1	1.50		11.2	24.8
CtyLonInv..	328	-2.1	24	1.5	88.1	5.10
CloseBrs ...	631.50	+3.0	40	0.7	925.8	12.10
CollStewH..	49.75	-1.7	3	2.2	123.4	2.11
El Oro	120xd	-13.7	3.33		77.6	2.11
Evolutn...◆	83.75	+12.4	2.75		194.9	10.8
F&C As....	68.50	+6.2	3		364.5	5.10
GlobeOp..†	267	-4.6	4.50	5.1	282.1	14.9
GuinPeat ..†	29.75	+2.6	1.15	2.3	482.7	7.9
Hargr Lans	468.50	+10.0	18.87	1.0	2,222.2	7.9
HenderGp.†	117.20	+14.9	5.85	2.0	1,285.6	31.8
ICAP.....†	369	+12.6	20.68	1.9	2,392.5	20.7
ICG........	244.60xd	+8.8	18	2.1	977.4	30.11
IFG........†	90xd	-2.7	4.15c	2.3	113.1	30.11
IG Group ..	481.80	+12.6	20	1.7	1,750.1	7.9
Indvardn 9tr.	783.10	+14.2	4		922.0	6.5
Investec ...	372.50	+12.8	17	2.4	2,022.6	27.7
IPF ....†	205.50	+20.8	6.74	3.2	528.6	7.9
Jupiter ....†	226.50	+12.4	7.20	2.3	1,036.7	31.8
Liontrust ..	77.25	+1.8			28.7	12'09
Lon Fin....	22		0.60	11.3	6.9	2.11
LSE.......†	851	+5.5	27.30	2.9	2,307.1	27.7
Man	142.40xd	+13.7	24.44c	0.9	2,631.0	23.11
Paragon...q	187.60	+5.3	4	5.0	561.1	29.6
Provident..†	997	+2.1	64.80	1.3	1,365.7	2.11
RathbnBr ..†	£10.82	+4.4	45	1.3	470.8	14.9
Record ....†	14xd	-5.1	3.34	0.9	31.0	30.11
Resolutn..†	253.10	+8.8	19.04	4.3	3,483.1	7.9
RSM Tenon.	15.25	-10.3	0.55	4.2	49.2	12.10
S&U......†	600	-2.4	37	1.8	70.5	12.10
Schroder .†	£13.83	+14.8	39	3.2	3,125.9	10.8
N/V....... †	£11.42	+10.6	39	3.2	639.3	10.8
TullettPre..	308	+7.4	15.75	3.1	663.2	26.10
WlkrCrip...	44.50xd		2.74	1.2	16.2	23.11

Food & Beverages

Notes	Price	Wks% Chg	Div	Cov	Mcap £m	Last xd
AngloEst ...	645	-0.4	5.56c	29.3	255.0	25.5
AscBrFd ...	£11.16	+2.9	24.75	2.8	8,835.1	8.6
Barr(AG) ..†	£11.77	+5.0	25.96	2.5	458.1	5.10
Britvic....q	329.40	+2.0	17.70	1.5	795.2	8.6
C&C€.......†	256.12xd	+10.1	6.97c	3.3	865.9	26.10
Carr'sMill..q	759	-2.1	26	3.1	67.3	14.9

Industrial Engineering

Notes	Price	Wks% Chg	Div	Cov	Mcap £m	Last xd
Bodycote..†	274.70	+11.5	9.35	2.9	525.4	5.10
Castines .†	278.50	-3.1	10.95	3.2	171.5	20.7
CharterInt|◆	935	+0.8	23.50	2.8	1,562.3	3.8
Fenner ....q	390	+6.6	8	3.2	754.3	27.7
Goodwin...	£10.28	-1.0	29.17	1.7	74.0	14.9
Hill&Sm ..†	249.50xd	+6.2	12.90	1.6	192.0	23.11
IMI ....†	778.50	+8.6	28	2.5	2,499.5	7.9
Melrose ..†	345	+7.1	13.51	1.8	1,348.8	7.9
Molins	92	-0.5	5	4.6	18.6	14.9
MS Intl ....†	305	+3.4	7	4.9	56.7	29.6
OMZ $.....	220.13	-0.9			78.1	
Renold	27.50	+2.8			60.4	
Rotork	£18.39xd	+11.5	34.25	2.4	1,594.3	16.11
SeverfdR .†	173		4	1.9	154.4	5.10
SKF Skr ...	£13.53	+20.1	5	2.7	5,578.3	29.4
Spirax-S....	£18.71	+7.3	44.80	2.7	1,453.0	12.10
Tex.......†	67.50		2.50	5.3	4.3	14.9
Trifast.....	38.88	+2.3			33.1	11'08
Vitec .....†	600.50	+0.9	19.40	1.9	259.7	28.9
Weir .....†	£20.74	+15.5	28.20	3.7	4,383.2	5.10

Industrial General

Notes	Price	Wks% Chg	Div	Cov	Mcap £m	Last xd
Barlowid R..	589.92	+11.4	155c	3.1	1,362.0	6.6
BritPoly ..†	325.25	-2.0	11.85	4.0	86.2	19.10
Cookson...†	490.40	+8.3	18.75	3.3	1,355.6	14.9
Cosalt .....◆	0.18	-5.4			0.7	8'08
JardnMt $ |◆	£30.93	-2.1	$1.18	9.7	20,481.4	17.8
Jard Str $.|◆	£18.61	+0.8	21.50c	3.9	20,838.2	17.8
MacIrine...	19.75		1.55	1.3	22.7	21.9
REXAM ...†	345.40	+4.4	12.70	2.5	3,029.1	7.9
RPC .....†	350.20	+10.6	12.30	2.1	568.5	3.8
Smith DS...	201	+9.5	6.50	3.5	876.8	10.8
Smiths.....	953	+7.9	36.25	2.2	3,741.0	26.10
SmurfKap€.	396.65	+14.4			872.9	10'08

Industrial Transportation

Notes	Price	Wks% Chg	Div	Cov	Mcap £m	Last xd
Avation....q	112	+0.9	1	8.9	43.2	8.12
Braemar...	303.50xd	-9.0	26	1.3	64.0	23.11
BBA Aviat .†	176.50	+7.2	8.22	1.9	841.6	24.8
Clarkson ..†	£11.38	+6.4	48	2.4	216.2	14.9
Fisher J....†	480	-4.0	15.04	2.9	240.1	5.10
Flybe Grp...	67	+12.1			50.4	
Goldenpt ..†	72	-0.3	5.04	0.7	65.4	7.9
OceanWil...	£12.15	+3.4	42c	4.0	649.7	31.8
PostNL €...	212.38	+21.0	57c	7.7	833.2	22.2
Stobart.....	116xd	+3.6	6	1.3	404.3	9.11
UK Mail.....	203.50xd	-1.9	18.20	1.1	111.4	30.11
Wincantn..†	56	-16.7			64.2	8.12

Figure 3-1: This column from the *Financial Times* shows ordinary shares listed according to their business sectors. It also shows the market capitalisation (in the column labelled 'Mcap £m') of each company.

It important to know that there is no definitive or widely accepted consensus about the definition of some of the categories. A stock that is called an 'established-growth company' by one analyst may be a 'blue-chip stock' to another. Or what an analyst at a broking firm describes as a 'mid-cap company' may be a 'small-cap company' in a report issued by a third-party analytical vendor. The result among many outside the industry is confusion – and some scepticism. Therefore, the definitions and references provided below are those that you are most likely to encounter in the stock markets. Nonetheless, it is always prudent to check a specific company's or organisation's definition of the term.

Classified by Sector

In the *Financial Times*, ordinary shares are classified according to their business sector. This categorisation is based on the International Classification Benchmark (ICB) created by the FTSE and Dow Jones (DJ) Indices. Shares are divided into industries, sectors and subsectors. The major industry divisions and their related sectors are listed in Figure 3–1 below:

INDUSTRY	SUPERSECTOR	SECTOR	SUBSECTOR
Basic Materials	Basic Resources	Forestry & Paper	Forestry
			Paper
		Industry Metals & Mining	Aluminium
			Iron & Steel
			Nonferrous Metals
		Mining	Coal
			Diamonds & Gemstones
			General Mining

INDUSTRY	SUPERSECTOR	SECTOR	SUBSECTOR
			Gold Mining
			Platinum & Precious Metals
	Chemicals	Chemicals	Commodity Chemicals
			Specialty Chemicals
Consumer Goods	Automobiles & Parts	Automobiles & Parts	Automobiles
			Auto Parts
			Tyres
	Food & Beverages	Beverages	Brewers
			Distillers & Vintners
			Soft Drinks
		Food Producers	Farming & Fishing
			Food Products
	Personal & House-hold Goods	Household Goods & Home Construction	Durable Household Products
			Nondurable Household Products
			Furnishings
			Home Construction
		Leisure Goods	Consumer Electronics
			Recreational Products
			Toys
		Personal Goods	Clothing & Accessories
			Footwear
			Personal Products
		Tobacco	Tobacco
Consumer Services	Media	Media	Broadcasting & Entertainment
			Media Agencies
			Publishing
	Retail	Food & Drug Retailers	Drug Retailers
			Food Retailers & Wholesalers

INDUSTRY	SUPERSECTOR	SECTOR	SUBSECTOR
		General Retailers	Apparel Retailers
			Broadline Retailers
			Home Improvement Retailers
			Specialised Consumer Services
			Specialty Retailers
	Travel & Leisure	Travel & Leisure	Airlines
			Gambling
			Hotels
			Recreational Services
			Restaurants & Bars
			Travel & Tourism
Financials	Banks	Banks	Banks
	Financial Services	Equity Investment Instruments	Equity Investment Instruments
		Financial Services	Asset Managers
			Consumer Finance
			Investment Services
			Mortgage Finance
			Specialty Finance
		Nonequity Investment Instruments	Nonequity Investment Instruments
	Insurance	Life Insurance	Life Insurance
		Nonlife Insurance	Full Line Insurance
			Insurance Brokers
			Property & Casualty Insurance
			Reinsurance
	Real Estate	Real Estate Investment & Services	Real Estate Holding & Development
			Real Estate Services
		Real Estate Invesment Trusts	Industrial & Office REITs

INDUSTRY	SUPERSECTOR	SECTOR	SUBSECTOR
			Retail REITs
			Residential REITs
			Diversified REITs
			Specialty REITs
			Mortgage REITs
			Hotel & Lodging REITs
Health Care	Health Care	Health Care Equipment & Services	Health Care Providers
			Medical Equipment
			Medical Supplies
		Pharmaceuticals & Biotechnology	Biotechnology
			Pharmaceuticals
Industrials	Construction & Metals	Construction & Materials	Building Materials & Fixtures
			Heavy Construction
	Industrial Goods & Services	Aerospace & Defense	Aerospace
			Defense
		Electronic & Electrical Equipment	Electrical Components & Equipment
			Electronic Equipment
		General Industrials	Containers & Packaging
			Diversified Industrials
		Industrial Engineering	Commercial Vehicles & Trucks
			Industrial Machinery
		Industrial Transportation	Delivery Services
			Marine Transportation
			Railroads
			Transportation Services
			Trucking

THE STOCK MARKET EXPLAINED

INDUSTRY	SUPERSECTOR	SECTOR	SUBSECTOR
		Support Services	Business Support Services
			Business Training & Employment Agencies
			Financial Administration
			Industrial Suppliers
			Waste & Disposal Services
Oil & Gas	Oil & Gas	Alternative Energy	Alternative Fuels
			Renewable Energy Equipment
		Oil & Gas Producers	Exploration & Production
			Integrated Oil & Gas
		Oil Equipment, Services & Distribution	Oil Equipment & Services
			Pipelines
Technology	Technology	Software & Computer Services	Computer Services
			Internet
			Software
		Technology Hardware & Equipment	Computer Hardware
			Electronic Office Equipment
			Semiconductors
			Telecommunications Equipment
Telecommunications	Telecommunications	Fixed Line Telecommunications	Fixed Line Telecommunications
		Mobile Telecommunications	Mobile Telecommunications
Utilities	Utilities	Electricity	Alternative Electricity
			Conventional Electricity

INDUSTRY	SUPERSECTOR	SECTOR	SUBSECTOR
		Gas, Water & Multi-Utilities	Gas Distribution
			Multi-Utilities
			Water

Figure 3-2: A chart showing the industries, supersectors, sectors and subsectors in which shares are categorised by the International Classification Benchmark (ICB). The organisation of the listing in the *Financial Times* shown in Figure 3-2 is based on the alphabetisation of selected sectors listed in the third column.

© FTSE International Limited 2010

http://www.icbenchmark.com/Site/ICB_Structure

Classified by Capitalisation

The size of the company is known as its *capitalisation* (or *market cap*). This is determined by multiplying the total number of issued-and-outstanding ordinary shares by their current market price per share. It's really that simple. Shares are therefore categorised as:

- Mega-cap: over £5 billion
- Large-cap: over £500 million to £5 billion
- Mid-cap: over £25 million to £500 million
- Small-cap: over £1 million to £25 million
- Micro-cap: £1 million or less

The numbers associated with each capitalisation category are not set in stone and can vary among market data companies, brokerage firms and ratings agencies. Not even the London Stock Exchange or FTSE have hard-and-fast values for each category. Also, keep in mind that as a company's financial conditions and consequently its share price change over time, its capitalisation will increase or decrease. Indices or unit trusts that focus on a particular capitalisation segment periodically remove and replace stocks at set periods due to changes in the company's total value.

Classified by the Stage of the Company's Development or Growth
Ordinary shares are frequently categorised according to where the company is in its development or growth. These classifications include:

- *Blue-chip stocks*. These are shares of large, usually multinational companies that have maintained market share as well as profits and earnings growth over many years and through various economic conditions. Blue-chip stocks tend to pay steady dividends and increase the amount periodically. The phrase 'blue chip' is a reference to the most valuable chip in a poker game.
- *Income stock*. These are companies that reliably pay a high percentage of their earnings as dividends. These are companies in mature industries where turnover is relatively consistent and growth is slow. Utility companies generally fall into this category. Because these shares do not offer the opportunity for substantial capital growth, the Boards of Directors of such companies understand that the shareholders buy and hold the shares for the reliability and regularity of the substantial dividend payments.
- *Growth stocks*. Shares referred to as growth stocks are frequently in new business areas that are expanding rapidly. These companies typically pay little or no dividends. Instead, the company reinvests its earnings in product development, research, marketing, human capital and expansion. Investors who buy growth stocks hope to make money from capital growth as the

share price rises in response to increases in company profits and earnings year after year. If the company is in a totally new business area that's attracting lots of media and investor attention and is seeing its market share or sales increase seemingly exponentially, it is widely referred to as an *emerging-growth company* or an *aggressive-growth company*. If the company whose shares have traded on the stock exchange for several years has continued to introduce or acquire new, successful products and is likely to begin paying a small or modest dividend, its ordinary shares would be described as an *established-growth company*. Many of these companies eventually become blue-chip stock. As you will have noticed in the previous sentences, the share description is also applied to the company.

- *Penny stock*. Valued at less than £1, these are cheap, highly speculative shares of small, emerging businesses or ordinary shares of once-high-flying companies whose businesses are going through difficult times. Many investors are attracted to these shares because of their inexpensive – sometimes thought of as bargain – prices. Investors frequently rationalise that the share price is so low that it can only go up. In reality, it can drop all the way to zero, and the entire amount invested could be lost. Penny shares are more risky than many investors are willing to admit.

Classified by the Reaction to Changes in the Economy

An economic cycle has four phases: expansion, prosperity, recession and recovery. There is no set time period for the length of each phase. A well-diversified portfolio consists of shares that react differently to economic changes. Understanding these groupings gives investors an additional tool to use in the prudent pursuit of diversification.

- *Cyclical shares.* These company shares benefit during prosperous economic times and decline in value during periods of economic contraction. In short, the company's turnover and profits, as well as its share price, move in tandem with the phases of the economic cycle. Shares of property companies are a prime example of cyclical shares. Companies in this sector were high flyers when the economy was doing well. As the economy contracted during the recession, they declined in value, moving almost in lock step with the economic cycle.
- *Countercyclical shares.* These shares do well when the economy contracts and don't fare so well when the economy expands. In short, their value moves opposite to changes in the economic cycle. The 'basics' that people revert to spending money on during tough economic times fall into this group. As a result, sales of companies producing these items rise, while those producing goods that represent mid-market luxury or discretionary purchases see their turnover and share prices decline. As the economy begins to improve, people will gradually spend less money on basics, choosing items that represent convenience instead. Other businesses that are considered countercyclical are gold mining companies, pawn shops, and credit collection companies.
- *Defensive shares.* These companies' businesses are somewhat cushioned against changes in the economy because they produce goods or supply services that people must buy or will want to buy through good

times and difficult times. They might buy a less expensive or generic version of the item, but they will continue to spend the money because the goods or services are regarded as a necessity. Shares of companies in the pharmaceutical, utility, and alcohol beverage sectors are good examples of defensive shares.

- *Interest-sensitive shares.* These are the shares of companies whose turnover and profits are affected by interest rate changes. Shares of banks and financial services companies are prime examples, as are businesses that depend on heavy amounts of borrowing. When interest rates are low, bank profits and share prices have historically increased. They can borrow money at a low rate and loan it out at a higher rate, capturing the difference as profit. As interest rates rise, bank profits might be adversely affected because the demand for loans from businesses is likely to decline at the same time. Thus profit margins on loans shrink. A bank's turnover, profits and share price are likely to decline or stay flat. However, a financial services company holding a substantial amount of assets in cash would see interest income rise. This may benefit the price of its shares. In general, low interest rates are good for the profits and share prices of banks and companies that depend on borrowing, whereas rising and high interest rates are thought to reduce profits, resulting in lower share prices.

As you've probably already concluded, one company's shares may occupy several classifications at one time. The ordinary shares in the consumer goods sector may be called a large-cap, defensive, blue-chip company, while the shares of a young company in the property development sector may be described as a small-cap, interest-sensitive, emerging-growth company. These thumbnail descriptions are useful because they give an investor a simple indication of the risk/return profile of a particular company or group of companies. The shares of a blue-chip, large-cap company are likely to be less volatile, pay dividends regularly, and provide reasonably steady, although rarely spectacular, capital growth over time. On the other hand, the shares of a small-cap, interest-sensitive property development firm are likely to be volatile and pay little or no dividend; they also offer the chance for price rises that are likely to make you think your dreams of quick riches through investment are within your easy grasp, as well as price declines that may feel like a punch in the gut. These thumbnail descriptions also give you a snapshot of the diversification or lack of diversification of the portfolio of equities that you may already own or are considering creating for yourself.

Risks and Rewards of Ordinary Shares

When investing in ordinary shares, one must be aware of both the potential risks and the potential rewards. Most people focus on the latter rather than the former, which can emotionally blind them to the very real downside of investing in shares. There are two significant risks. The worst is that the company goes bankrupt. As an ordinary shareholder your equity in the company would be totally worthless and the likelihood of your getting any money from the liquidation process is virtually zero. Remember: common shareholders are at the bottom of the list in terms of claims on a company's assets in a liquidation.

The second risk is that the shares underperform

against both your expectations and the overall market as measured by a broad-based index like the FTSE 100. It is when this underperformance results in a loss that an investor faces a dilemma that is often emotionally tinged: whether to sell the shares and realise the loss, or continue to hold them, hoping for a price recovery to at least your break-even price. Once one's emotions become entangled with an investment, the likelihood of making a poor decision increases, thereby exacerbating what could already be an unfortunate financial situation.

The potential rewards of ordinary shares are straightforward. The first is price appreciation – that the value of the shares will rise significantly and produce a gain, either somewhat satisfyingly small or blissfully large. For most people who buy and hold ordinary shares long-term, the reward is seeing their wealth increase as the prices rise. For those who trade actively, they are happy as long as the realised capital gains exceed any realised capital losses, leaving them with a net profit. Most achieve this by quickly cutting their losses on losing trades and letting their profits run on winning trades.

The next reward of ordinary shares is directly related to price appreciation. If the price of the company's ordinary shares becomes very high (a relative term), then its Board of Directors may choose to split the stock. For the person who already owns the company's stock, the split means that he or she will own more shares at a lower cost-basis per share. A split lowers the market price per share making it more attractive to the average investor. It also increases liquidity because there are more shares outstanding. If the company's shares continue to appreciate after the split, investors will own more shares on which to make capital gains.

And the third reward of ordinary shares is dividend payments. For long-established companies with a history of regular and increasing dividend payments, this is a feature that makes them attractive to many investors. However, these large, successful companies tend to grow more slowly. This is reflected in the price movement of their shares, which tends to be less volatile and rise more slowly. A younger company may need to reinvest its profit in itself and therefore pays no dividends during the early stages of its development. Investors will make profits solely from the capital growth of the company's shares if it becomes more and more successful. However, as the company's profits increase, its Board of Directors can eventually elect to begin paying dividends and also increase the amount periodically.

While investing in ordinary shares involves what I like to call 'research-supported optimism' about the future price movement, it is always prudent to keep the risks in mind and avoid letting your emotions cloud your clear view of those dangers as well as the potential rewards.

Preference Shares

[Note: This type of security is seldom issued in the UK today and only a few are still listed on the London Stock Exchange. This section will help you understand those that are available in the market. Additionally, one can never tell when a type of security will become popular again with companies and investors due to economic or legislative changes.]

Sometimes called *preferred stock*, a *preference share* is an equity security that has, as its name states, 'preference' over ordinary shares in two specific situations. The first is the receipt of dividend payments. If a dividend-paying company has issued preference shares, it must pay the money to holders of preference shares before it can pay any money to ordinary shareholders.

The second 'preference' involves the liquidation process when a business goes bankrupt or is wound up. A preference shareholder has claims on the company's remaining assets ahead of ordinary shareholders. In reality, this means very little. It's highly unusual for any shareholder, preference or ordinary, to get money back when a company liquidates. In return for these preferences, holders of preference shares have no voting rights and therefore no say in company matters such as the election of the Board of Directors. They are essentially silent equity owners in a business.

Dividends are different on preference shares. While all dividends must be declared by a company's Board of Directors and are usually paid every six months, the amount of the payment on a preference share is fixed. The dividend rate is stated as an annual fixed percentage based on a stated principal amount of the preferred, *not* the market value of the preferred. The dividend does not increase as the company's profits and earnings increase. If the company's profitability and earnings decline, the Board can suspend all dividend payments on all equity securities, including preference shares. Therefore, the dividend payment is *not* guaranteed, which is a common misconception.

Given the basic features just discussed, it's clear that preference shares have a lot in common with bonds, except that all types of shares have an indefinite life, while bonds and other fixed-income securities have a set maturity date. The similarity to bonds means that preference shares appeal to a different type of investor, typically one who is more conservative and who is interested in capital preservation with modest growth, rather than capital growth and its inherent volatility.

Features of Preference Shares

To make its preference shares attractive to investors, a company will give these securities certain characteristics to make them more marketable to the intended purchasers. Frequently in newspapers and magazines, as well as on websites, these are referred to as 'types' of preference shares. It would be more accurate to refer to these as 'features' of preference shares. When issuing the shares, companies decide what one feature or combination of features will make people interested in buying the shares. Some of the features benefit the company and others benefit the shareholder. Five of the most common features are explained below.

Cumulative (usually abbreviated *Cum Pref*)

If a company misses a dividend payment on its cumulative preference shares or cannot pay the dividend in full, then the missed amount accrues – i.e. is added – to the amount of the next payment. No dividends can be paid to ordinary shareholders until the company pays all of the missed, accrued dividends to the holders of the cumulative preference shares. Importantly, the company pays no interest on the missed, unpaid dividends. If the dividend accrues separately from the price of the preference shares, the security is said to trade 'clean'. If, however, the dividend builds up in the market value of the shares, the security is said to trade 'dirty'. In this second case, the market value of the shares will drop on the day the dividend is paid. (In the industry this is known as the *ex-dividend date* – i.e. the date when the shares trade without the embedded dividend.) A preference share without the cumulative feature is called noncumulative, usually abbreviated *Non Cum Pref*.

Callable

This feature gives the company the right to buy back its preference shares at a stated price during specific periods of time. Issuers of preference shares are most likely to exercise a call feature when interest rates, and therefore dividend rates, are going down. When a company does this, it calls (i.e. retires) the preference shares on which it is paying a high dividend. It may simultaneously issue new preference shares with a lower dividend rate. Calls are never to the investor's advantage. So, to make the call feature somewhat palatable to investors, companies usually issue these shares with a period of *call protection*. This is a specified period of time, starting on the issue date, when the company cannot forcibly retire (call) its preference shares. Investors therefore know the time during which they can reasonably count on receiving the fixed dividend. A preference share without a call feature is referred to as a noncallable.

Redeemable (abbreviated *Red Pref*)

This is another term used for callable preference shares. A share without this characteristic is also referred to as irredeemable.

Convertible

The holder of preference shares with this feature has the right to convert to a fixed number of ordinary shares at a fixed price that's based on the principal amount (not the market price) of the underlying security. A holder of a preference share with a £100 par value, for example, may have the right to convert to ten ordinary shares. The conversion price of each ordinary share would be £10 [£100 ÷ 10]. If the market price of the ordinary shares languishes below the set conversion price (£10 in the example above), the preference shareholder won't convert but will receive the stated fixed dividend. If, however, the market price of the ordinary shares rises significantly above the conversion price (£10) then the shareholder will convert from preference stock to ordinary shares and would no longer receive the fixed dividend. Thus, the shareholder would now be able to participate in the company's anticipated capital growth. The other scenario in which the holder of a convertible preferred might convert is when the dividend payments on the ordinary shares became materially higher than those on the convertible. Even though the investor might have lost a bit of money at conversion, that loss would be recouped in a reasonable period of time by the ordinary shares' higher dividend. Therefore the investor would be receiving a better return over the long-term.

Convertible preference shares are often referred to as a *hybrid security* because it has traits of both equity securities and fixed-income securities. Because it offers both the right to receive a fixed dividend and the opportunity to participate in the company's capital growth through conversion, a convertible preference share pays a lower dividend than other types of preference shares. [Note:

Other types of convertible securities, like convertible corporate bonds, work essentially the same way.]

Variable Rate

The dividend rate on preference shares with this feature is periodically reset up or down, based on the movement of a benchmark interest rate like LIBOR (the London Interbank Offer Rate). This feature tends to lower the volatility of the preference shares because the new rate reflects those available in the market as well as the financial condition of the issuer at the time of the reset. The period when the dividend percentage is adjusted varies – some as short as six months, some annually. There is no standard for all variable rate preference shares. It depends on what the issuer thinks will make the securities attractive to investors.

Risks and Rewards of Preferred Stock

As with any equity security, the principal risk is that the company goes bankrupt and the preference shares are worthless. The fact that these shares have preference ahead of ordinary shares when a company liquidates – a fact that is widely touted suggesting that it offers some safety or protection – means little to nothing. As a practical matter, wages, taxes and all bondholders must be paid before money can be distributed to preference shareholders. If all of those with claims ahead of preference shareholders don't receive 100% of the money they are due as the company's assets are liquidated, then the preference shareholders will receive nothing. This is what usually happens.

Receiving a fixed dividend means that the preference shareholder does not participate in the company's capital growth. This risk is made stark when a business is growing and becoming more profitable and the price of its ordinary shares rises. Additionally, the company may decide to increase the size of its dividends to ordinary shareholders. In contrast, preference shareholders would see no change in their dividend payments and would most likely see the market value of their shares stay relatively flat, trading around the shares' principal value.

Because the dividend on most preference shares is fixed, this security is subject to interest rate risk – exactly the same as bonds. As interest rates rise, the market price of preference shares will decline. And as interest rates fall, the market price of preference shares will rise. The value of preference shares could decline not because there has been any fundamental change in the future prospects or profitability of the company that issued them, but solely based on an increase in interest rates. The lower the dividend rate on the preferred, the more adversely it will be affected by any increase in interest rates.

Purchasing power risk is also associated with preference shares. This is the risk that, over time, the money you earn from the fixed dividend payments will be able to buy fewer goods and services in the marketplace. If the economy enters an inflationary period where the cost of everything from basic foods and household appliances to cars and holiday travel is rising, the amount of these items each fixed dividend payment could purchase would shrink, perhaps severely. While investors in preference shares may be concerned about preservation of capital, by being too conservative they may be subject to a decline in the real value of the money they are trying to keep safe. Another name for purchasing power risk is *inflation risk*.

The two rewards of preference shares are regular

dividend income and preservation of capital. Preference shares are issued primarily by companies that have strong, consistent cash flows. These include blue-chip companies, banks, financial services companies and utilities. Issuers must have enough earnings to pay dividends to both preference shareholders and ordinary shareholders. [Note: A company would not issue preference shares if it did not have enough earnings to also pay dividends on its ordinary shares. Such a move would make the ordinary shareholders angry and this would most likely be strongly expressed at the next annual meeting and election of the Board of Directors.]

Summary

While ordinary shares and preference shares are both categorised as equities, they have only two traits in common: 1) an indefinite life when they are issued, and 2) the right (not a guarantee) to receive dividends. For ordinary shareholders, most of their other rights – i.e. to vote, to maintain proportionate ownership, claims following a bankruptcy – are typically part of the company's Articles of Association. At most, a company might have two classes of ordinary shares issued and outstanding: one class with full or disproportionately large voting rights, and another class with limited or no voting rights. However, this practice is not common or viewed positively in the UK. Preference share features (e.g. dividend rate, cumulative, convertible) are decided issue by issue, according to what will make that offering most marketable to the potential shareholders given the condition of the company's financial situation and/or the conditions in the overall economy.

Because ordinary shares reflect different aspects of the issuing company's development, its reaction to the economy, and the investor's desire for capital growth, income or both, this type of equity security can appeal to a wide range of investors with different investment objectives. All of these varying and uncertain factors point to the greater risk associated with ordinary shares. It is fair to say that preference shares appeal to a more conservative investor who is interested in steady income (from dividends), low volatility and preservation of capital. This difference is underscored by the fact that preference shares are usually included in a brokerage firm's fixed-income department. Also, newspapers, magazines and websites frequently describe preference shares as 'a widow and orphans security', an outdated reference to the traditionally low-risk profile of the typical public investor for this type of equity security.

4

Analysis: Fundamental and Technical

The collective price movement of shares is widely viewed as a leading economic indicator. It is believed to indicate strongly which phase of the business cycle – i.e. expansion, prosperity, recession and recovery – the overall economy is heading towards. For example, when stock prices start moving lower and lower despite occasional rallies, it could indicate that business profits will be slowing in the future, which could in turn cause the economy to slide into a recession. Conversely, if stock prices begin to show an overall upward trend, it could be a sign that the economy is heading towards a recovery.

One of the questions I like to ask in virtually every class I teach is, 'What causes prices of shares to move up and down every day?' Before anyone answers, I add that they are not permitted to use the phrase 'supply and demand'. This almost invariably brings forth quizzical looks on people's faces, followed by a long, searching silence.

While 'supply and demand' is the correct response in the broadest sense, a more accurate answer to the question would be 'investors' expectations'. People, both retail and institutional investors, buy and sell shares based on expectations about 1) the future price movement and/or growth of the company, its business sector, or the overall market; 2) the possible increase (or decrease) in the rate of inflation; and 3) the impact that global events may have on domestic markets around the world. These expectations are created and supported using analysis.

There are two approaches to analysing shares for investment: *fundamental analysis* and *technical analysis*. Fundamental analysis examines the financial statements of the company itself to see if, either on their own merit or in comparison to other companies in the same business sector, the company has strong or weak growth prospects. Will turnover and profits continue to increase consistently? How will they be affected by competition and changes in economic conditions? Does the company have too much debt? Fundamental analysis is also used to determine if a company's shares are undervalued (i.e. the market price is too low relative to the company's or its competitors' profits and earnings growth) and therefore likely to rise in price, or are overvalued (i.e. priced too high relative to profits and earnings growth) and are likely to fall in price. Fundamental analysis tries to determine the price movement of shares over the intermediate to long-term.

Technical analysis, on the other hand, uses charts of past price movement of individual stocks, as well as the overall market (as measured by broad-based indices), to predict future movement. The many tools of technical analysis can sound like a description of a Picasso painting – rounded top, double bottom, inverted head and shoulders – combined with terms such as 'sentiment indicators' that might be used in a group therapy session. The belief underlying this second approach is that investors, both institutional and retail, tend to act in unison (this is called the *herd mentality*) and tend to repeat behaviour patterns in response to changes in the market. Charting a stock's or the market's movement reveals the patterns, and therein lay the profit-making or loss-avoiding opportunities. Technical analysis is typically used for short- to intermediate-term investment strategies.

Although fundamental and technical analysis are quite different, many investors combine aspects of the two to help affirm or give more support to a particular outlook about an individual's stock's performance or the movement of the overall market.

Fundamental Analysis

Fundamental analysis examines the many ratios and measures of a company's financial condition and future prospects. It's about 'crunching the numbers', a phrase that arouses anxiety in the stomachs of many people or causes others to want to move quickly to another topic. For an investor with little or no experience in the market, the measures can seem like a miasma of abbreviations and acronyms – EPS, P-E ratio, EBITDA, ROI, ROE, P-B ratio, and others.

In reality, it is easier to understand the basic, essential measures of fundamental analysis than all of the technical terms, abbreviations and jargon would suggest. You don't have to have an MBA or be a mathematics whiz. At the bottom line it's numerical common sense.

There are five measures used in fundamental analysis that, I believe, every investor should understand, whether you're beginning as an investor or whether you have some experience. These have not been selected arbitrarily. They are based on what you're likely to hear financial market analysts discuss on television, radio and websites, as well as in newspapers and magazines; what successful industry professionals say they consider when deciding to buy or sell a stock, and what my experience (as well as that of my friends and colleagues) tells me are the measures to which you need pay close attention. Having a basic understanding of these concepts and numbers will help you construct a solid foundation on which you should be able to make well-supported investment decisions and, equally importantly, learn additional, often more complex information easily when you need it or want it.

1. Earnings Per Share (EPS) and Earnings Growth

Most analysts believe that a company's earnings are the central influence on the price movement of its ordinary shares. Investors buy or sell stock in anticipation of a company's current and future earnings. The importance of this fundamental analytical tool is underscored by the fact that television channels devoted to financial news highlight the beginning of the 'earnings season'. This is the period during which groups of important companies announce their much-anticipated earnings per share. Analyst at brokerage firms and research companies spend a lot of time and money attempting to predict a company's earnings and deduce what it means for the future of its business.

Earnings and profits are not synonyms. *Earnings* are the portion of the company's turnover or gross revenues that remain after it has paid all operating expenses (including extraordinary charges), bond interest and taxes. The resulting net amount is the company's earnings after taxes. If the company has preference shares outstanding, the Board will declare the fixed dividend on those shares. [Note: Dividends on cumulative preference shares are deducted whether or not they are declared because the company must pay all of the missed dividends before it can pay any dividends to ordinary shareholders.]

After the preference dividend is deducted from the earnings after taxes, this leaves the company with the all-important earnings for ordinary shares. This is the total amount of money available to be paid to the ordinary shareholder. The EPS are then calculated by dividing the earnings for ordinary shares by the weighted average of the outstanding shares during the period of time for which the earnings are being calculated. [Note: Some firms use the number of ordinary shares outstanding on the last day of the period.]

$$\textit{Earnings per Share (EPS)} = \frac{\textit{Net Income After Taxes} - \textit{Preference Dividend}}{\textit{Weighted Average of Ordinary Outstanding Shares}}$$

or

$$\textit{Earnings per Share (EPS)} = \frac{\textit{Total Earnings for Common}}{\textit{Weighted Average of Outstanding Ordinary Share}}$$

A company may report its earnings in three ways: primary EPS, fully diluted EPS, or earnings before interest, taxes, depreciation and amortisation (commonly referred to by the acronym EBITDA).

- *Primary EPS*. This earnings figure is calculated using as its denominator or divisor the weighted average of all ordinary shares outstanding in the stock market for the given earnings period, or the number of shares outstanding on the day at the end of the period when the calculation is done.
- *Fully Diluted EPS*. The calculation of this figure adds to the denominator the total of all the additional ordinary shares that would be outstanding if securities, such as convertible bonds, convertible preference shares, warrants and company-issued stock options to management and employees were converted into outstanding ordinary shares. Many analysts consider this to be a more realistic assessment of a company's earnings, since these other securities could become outstanding ordinary shares at any moment.
- *EBITDA (Earnings Before Interest, Taxes, Depreciation and Amortisation)*. The name says exactly what is added back into a more traditional calculation of EPS. The advantage of EBITDA is that it reports the earnings figure before it is distorted by the creative accounting and other financial practices a company may use. EBITDA is also referred to as *operational cash flow*. This earnings figure is most often reported by companies with a large amount of intangible assets such as copyrights or a brand-name company it owns, or assets on their books whose value they can write down (i.e. amortise) over time. EBITDA is sometimes reported by companies that are highly leveraged, i.e. have large amounts of debt outstanding.

Predicting a company's earnings per share for the upcoming period (usually every six months) is one of the major objectives of stock analysts at different firms – and it is not without controversy. Their predictions and justifications about whether the earnings will increase or decrease are compared to the same period during the previous year, *not* the previous six months. This information is available on many investment websites and discussed on news programmes.

The analysts' collective predictions can have a strong impact on investors' actions, both in anticipation of the company's announcement and on the day the actual EPS is made public. If earnings significantly exceed expectations and the analysts believe the trend is likely to continue, investors will buy the companies' ordinary shares, driving the price higher. If earnings fall short of the analysts' consensus, investors will sell shares, trying to get out of the market before the prices fall. Their actions drive the price lower.

It is equally important to look at the increasing or decreasing trend of a company's earnings per share. Steadily increasing earnings per share usually means the company is growing and that its financial condition is improving. If the increase is due to a corresponding improvement in turnover and profits, then the business is growing. Over time, the shares should rise as the company becomes more valuable.

Increasing EPS are not always the result of increasing turnover or profits. The company may be buying back its own stock. This strategy is typically implemented when its share price is unusually low and it has huge amounts of cash reserves. The stock buy-back programme reduces the number of shares outstanding. Depending on the number of shares repurchased, the effect could be an increase in the EPS, even as turnover, profits and/or earnings stay flat or decline. If this increase in EPS proves temporary and is not supported by corresponding increases in revenues and profits, investors will lose confidence in the company and begin unloading the shares.

A decrease in EPS is generally a negative indicator. Generally, lower EPS are the result of lower turnover, higher costs, and thus lower profits. There are some key things to look for both within and outside the company that could cause lowered EPS, which may be only temporary. One internal factor could be a stock split or the payment of a stock dividend, instead of a cash dividend. Both of these corporate actions result in a significant increase in the number of ordinary shares outstanding; thus, the earnings per share would decline. Keep in mind that a stock split and a stock dividend are usually viewed as positive developments, especially if there is no decrease in the total earnings for ordinary shares.

External factors that may affect a company's EPS are business conditions in a particular sector or the overall economy. Perhaps the majority of businesses in the same sector are experiencing a downturn in turnover and profits. This is what happened in the banking sector beginning in late 2007. Also, the overall economy could be in a recession with businesses experiencing lower earnings. In this case, the decrease in EPS may be characteristic of this particular phase of the business cycle and the EPS do not, therefore, provide a good long-term view of the growth prospects of that specific company.

2. Price-Earnings Ratio (P-E)

This ratio measures the market price of one ordinary share of a company's stock, relative to its earnings per share (EPS). The formula is simple:

$$Price\text{-}Earnings\ Ratio = \frac{Current\ Market\ Price}{Earnings\ Per\ Share}$$
$$(P\text{-}E)$$

In simple terms, the P-E ratio tells an analyst or investor how expensive a company's share price is compared to its earnings. Stated another way, the P-E ratio indicates how many times or multiples a stock's price is trading above its earnings. If, for example, a share has a market price of 800p and its EPS are 40p, then the company's P-E ratio is 20 [800p ÷ 40p]. The company's shares are trading at a price that is 20 times its earnings. To understand what this number means for an individual company, its current P-E ratio is compared to its historical P-E ratios, to those of other companies in the same sector, and to that of the overall market as measured by a broad market index, such as the FTSE 100.

Clearly, a young company in a fast-growing industry may not have earnings and therefore will have a denominator of zero in the formula above. Such a company will have no P-E ratio. This easy and simple insight is a good place to begin understanding how P-E ratios are interpreted in the stock market. A high P-E ratio is indicative of an emerging or aggressive growth company. Investors are willing to pay a high market price today for the stock because they are very bullish on the company's future growth, even though it currently has little or no earnings. Think about some of today's big technology and Internet and social companies first debuted on the stock market. Their P-E ratios were astronomical at the time. However, some of these companies' increasing profitability finally yielded higher earnings and therefore lowered P-E ratios, while others crashed, never realising their potential.

If a more established company has a high P-E ratio compared to other businesses in the same sector, or in the overall stock market, this is interpreted to mean the company's shares are overvalued – the share price is too high and is likely to decline. A speculative investor might sell short in anticipation in order to profit from the decline. Overall, regardless of how an analyst interprets a high P-E ratio, it is generally believed to be an indicator of higher volatility and risk.

A low P-E ratio is characteristic of companies in mature, slow-growth industries. Supermarket chains, pharmaceuticals and utilities are examples of these. Many blue-chip companies have low ratios. These corporations have strong, consistent earnings, part of which they may choose to pay to shareholders as dividends. While some people see a low P-E ratio as an indication of a stable investment, others see it as an indication that a company's stock price is too low. In short, the shares are undervalued. This could be caused by temporary market conditions that have little to do with the actual value of the company. A value-oriented investor would buy the shares and wait for them to reach a market price that his or her research shows them to be fully and fairly valued. At that point the investor might sell them.

Analysts also examine the collective P-E ratios of all stocks in the FTSE 100 index, for example. If the overall P-E ratio of the index is low, this could be an indication that the market is reaching a bottom and that an intermediate-to-long-term rally may occur. If the market's P-E ratio is high, this could mean the market is reaching a peak and is likely to decline soon. If an investor owned the shares, he or she could sell them to capture the gain before the drop. A more speculative strategy (if he or she did not own the shares) would be to sell them short in order to profit from the anticipated price decline and eventually buy them back when they came close to their low point.

Like each of the fundamental measures discussed in this section, a company's current P-E ratio should not be considered in isolation. Remember that to be useful, it must be interpreted in light of the business's historical P-E ratios, those of its peers, and that of the overall market. The information necessary to do these comparisons is available through your own brokerage firm and through many websites that provide up-to-date investment information and analysis.

3. Turnover and Profit

Turnover is the total amount of money coming into the company from its sales and other revenue sources before operating expenses and taxes have been deducted. Turnover is driven by unit volume (the quantity of goods and services a company sells) and price (the amount a company charges for such goods and services). Volume and price are each influenced by economic, industry and company-specific factors.

Pre-tax profit is the remaining turnover after operating expenses (which include rent or mortgage, cost of goods or raw materials, electricity, salaries, benefits, etc.) and interest have been deducted. When people use the term 'the bottom line', post-tax profit or earnings is what they are referring to. Turnover and profit should be evaluated separately in two ways: first, to understand the pattern of growth (or decline) over time, and second, to glean the meaning behind any changes in the margin of profits relative to turnover.

When evaluating turnover and profits in older, established companies, ideally you would like to see that both have been growing steadily over a number of years – the longer the better. To understand a company's current numbers in both of these categories, start with its annual report. Every public company must file an audited annual report with a stock exchange in order for its shares to remain listed and traded in the market. The report is also made available on the company's website.

You want to know what contributes to the total turnover – whether it is essentially from one product, from a few specialty items, or from a diverse portfolio of goods and services. Clearly a company with only one successful product or a few specialised products can become a huge moneymaking investment if the company is the leader in its sector or has a lock on its market. This occurs, most notably, with products and services that are relatively insensitive to shifts in consumer trends, such as medical devices and pharmaceutical products that satisfy unmet needs. However, such a narrow focus can prove risky in the consumer market where people's tastes change. We've seen examples of this in the mobile phone market, where once stalwart industry names are now struggling as users shift to the products of more innovative companies.

If there are any unusual spikes or drops in the pattern

of turnover and/or profits, investigate the cause. Reasons might be the successful introduction of a new product or service; costs involved in the acquisition and integration of a new company; disruption in the delivery of key components (as we saw with technology companies after the tsunami in Japan); the signing of a lucrative sales agreement; an upturn in the demand for that product in that business sector; seasonal factors; or a downturn in the economy. The key here is to determine if the aberration is likely to be temporary or ongoing. If a sharp but temporary turn in business causes a stock's market price to overreact either up or down, an investment opportunity may be staring you in the eyes. Likewise, if there is a muted reaction to a development that will have a long-term beneficial impact, there may be an opportunity to invest in an undervalued situation. The key is to figure out if the long-term impact will be more positive or negative.

If the change is related to the business sector or the economy, then compare it to the reported turnovers and profits of the company's peers to see if the company you're interested in was affected more, less, or the same as others. Then try to ascertain the reason for this difference, if there is one. This investigation, perhaps using published reports by analysts, will help you develop a sense of the comparative or relative risk that the company's finances may face as the business environment changes.

Many young companies in new growth areas may not have profits or earnings. This is because the company is investing any money it generates into its operations – areas like, research and development (R&D), new product creation, marketing and sales, hiring of key personnel, etc. In this situation, it's best to focus on the increase in turnover as well as the growth in market share. If both of these are consistently increasing, then the company should eventually become profitable. The pace and reliability of the rise in turnover will help you gauge the timing of the company's profitability.

The profit margin of a company is also an important measure to understand. This is calculated using a simple formula:

$$\text{Profit Margin} = \left(\frac{\text{Pre-Tax Profit}}{\text{Turnover}} \right) \times 100$$

This tells you what percentage of the company's total revenue or turnover remains after all the operational costs and interest on debts are deducted. The percentage of profit margin can signal how cost-efficiently a company is being run. This is one of the justifications that management may use for laying off employees, eliminating or reducing certain benefits, or selling selected assets when it acquires or merges with another business. By getting rid of the 'fat', the company is thought to be much more 'lean' (meaning more efficient), like a marathon runner. As a result, more of the top line (turnover) may drop to the bottom line (profits).

Increasing and decreasing profit margins can be due to factors other than cost-efficiency or the lack thereof. If, for example, the company has a product whose sales have skyrocketed, then an increase in the profit margin may come from the economies of scale that happen when more items are produced at a relatively fixed cost. For example, the cost to maintain property is rather stable and usually doesn't rise nearly as fast as the rents a landlord charges tenants. In this case, rising margins can be attributable to rising demand and prices, without regard to the property company's aptitude in controlling costs.

Alternatively, a lower profit margin may not be due to the company being poorly managed. Instead, it may be due to a single item or strategy, such as offering free shipping as part of a special holiday promotion. While this marketing effort may have been successful in increasing turnover, the volume of sales at the lower prices could be insufficient to cover all of the costs of the shipping and handling; hence, the company's profit margins are squeezed. This happens during the Christmas holiday season with some traditional brick-and-mortar retail stores as they seek to compete with Internet-only-based business.

In addition to understanding what causes changes in the profit margin of a specific company, it is important to look at the margin relative to its competitors. As stated earlier, this comparison will help you to understand if the percentage is typical of this business sector. It can also highlight advantages a company has over its competitors or challenging financial risks that management needs to address.

Turnover and profits are driving forces of a stock's price movement. Understanding each in their own right – and both as they relate to one another – is crucial. In doing so, an investor begins to appreciate the effects that economic conditions and corporate decision making (e.g. pricing decisions, investments in research and development, opening new locations, etc.) bring to bear on sales and the level of efficiency at which goods and services are produced, marketed, and distributed to generate profits.

If done properly, this will lead to earnings and gains for ordinary shareholders.

4. Dividend Yield

Dividends are that portion of a company's earnings that its Board of Directors decides to pay to ordinary shareholders. Most companies declare and pay dividends semi-annually, although some large companies pay quarterly. No company pays out all of its earnings as dividends. It retains part of the money (called *retained earnings*) so that it can meet its financial commitments and be financially flexible if some interesting opportunity comes along.

$$\text{Dividend Yield} = \left(\frac{\textbf{Annual Dividend Amount}}{\textbf{Current Market Price}} \right) \times 100$$

When the total annual dividend per share is divided by the share's current market price, the result is the *dividend yield*. It tells an investor what percentage the dividend represents of the share's current market price.

The weight an individual investor places on dividend yield when deciding to invest in a company's shares depends on whether his or her objective is for current income or long-term capital appreciation. For a person living off the dividend payments, it is of paramount importance, along with preservation of capital. Shares that have a high dividend yield are referred to as *dividend shares* or *income shares*. Websites like *The Motley Fool* or *Dividend Investor* regularly publish lists of companies that consistently pay significant dividends.

They are involved in industries like food, pharmaceuticals, petrol, consumer goods and utilities. A high dividend yield tends to be characteristic of mature, blue-chip companies – those in slow-growth industries with turnover that increases in line with, or slightly better than the growth of the economy. Because their prices tend to be rather stable, or fluctuate with the movement of the overall stock market, these types of businesses offer little opportunity for substantial capital gains. Therefore, to make themselves attractive to investors, their Boards of Directors decide to pay a substantial amount of their earnings as dividends. The risk of losing principal, while not eliminated, is less than it would be with more volatile shares.

For investors interested in capital appreciation, current yield will probably not be a significant factor when deciding which shares to buy or sell. Growth of turnover, profits and earnings will be more important considerations. This is clearly more risky because of the longer time horizon, even with the best research and analysis.

I have heard some investors say it is safer to take your cash returns today rather than wait and hope for the capital appreciation to produce the returns at some point in the future. Investors who think in such either/ or terms may be short-changing themselves. Perhaps, for most investors, the best approach is a combination of investing in the shares of companies that pay some dividends, which can be reinvested rather than used as cash, while simultaneously offering moderate opportunity for capital appreciation. This combination of dividend income and capital appreciation on an investment is known as the *total return*. Principal growth is as important as income and principal preservation if you do not want your investments and the buying power of your money to be undermined by inflation – which is always present to a lesser or greater degree in most economies.

The current yield of the overall market is often talked and written about by investment professionals. For example, they will cite the yield of the FTSE 100, an index of predominantly blue-chip shares, comparing it to interest that would be earned on corporate bonds or risk-free gilts. Because of the historically low volatility associated with the companies in this index, they are often thought of as reasonably safe investments. So, it would be logical to conclude that an investor who is willing to tolerate a little more risk by buying a diversified portfolio of shares that will approximate the return of the FTSE 100, or who purchases a tracker fund (explained in Chapter 6), he or she can get a higher return than on lower-risk fixed-income securities. However a look back at yields in the UK reveals a curious fact. For many decades equities yields have been half of gilt yields. That meant that the safer security paid you more. (Keep in mind, however, that although gilts are safer, they do not offer the opportunity for capital growth that ordinary shares do.) Today, the situation has reversed itself. Gross dividend yields (i.e. pre-tax) yields on equities have been higher than those on gilts. In this environment, the key question in your decision is: Are you willing and able to tolerate the higher risk for the higher dividend yield of the overall stock market?

5. Know the Business and the Quality of the Management

Warren Buffett holds to this principle and, based on my best and worst investment experiences, I believe it is essential to selecting a good long-term investment. This doesn't guarantee you'll be right all of the time. (Buffett surely hasn't been.) But using this approach increases the probability that you'll make a sound, well-reasoned decision. Regardless of what the numbers indicate, first and foremost you must understand how the company's business works and makes money. You should understand these fundamentals in a clear, simple and complete way that you can articulate to others, but most importantly to yourself. Being able to do this reaffirms that you know what you're buying. Some other issues that should be considered are:

- Is it a product you can understand and see why people would use or want it?
- Is the business based on a product or service that is essential to a definable group of customers?
- Is it a difficult business for competitors to enter?
- Is it a brand name associated with quality that will attract new customers as the business grows?

Also remember, it takes people (sometimes referred to today as 'human capital') to make an organisation run well and steer it successfully through always-changing business environments and economic conditions. Try to get an understanding of the company's management. Degrees from prestigious universities and business schools are no guarantee a person has the insight, vision, intuition or understanding of the business's customer base to create the short-term and long-term plan that a company needs to be successful today and build towards greater success in the future. Warren Buffett likes to say that he only buys companies that even a fool could run, because the chances are good that one day a fool will do so.

Summary

Many brokerage and financial services firms have their own analysts who cover specific sectors and produce regular reports for their customers that evaluate and discuss the five fundamental items covered above, and more. If you are a client of such a firm, their reports are a good source of information for gaining insight into a company's finances and its management. There are also third-party vendors, most notably Company Refs, that offer analytical information as a subscription service, either in bound form, on CD, or online. The last option is increasingly popular because it is updated daily with information from the London Stock Exchange. These third-party vendors look dispassionately at a company's financial statements and the actions of its management to offer users commentary and analysis that are not influenced by the company's public relations efforts. And finally, there are many websites – some objective, some not – where investors and a few self-proclaimed analysts publish their own interpretation of a company's numbers to share with other interested people. It may require a bit of sifting, but you just might find an independently run site that you like and find useful. It is always encouraging to have objective support for your view about a possible investment – just as it is useful to learn the logic held by those on the opposite side of (i.e. have a different point of view about) a trade you are considering. Therefore, regardless of your source of information, it's good to choose more than one provider as you reach your buy, sell, or hold decisions.

Technical Analysis

Technical analysis (often used as a synonym for the term *charting*) examines patterns of past price and volume movement to predict whether an individual stock or the overall market is likely to rise, decline or move sideways in the future. The underlying principle is that much of the stock market's movement is caused by investors' emotional reactions and these tend to repeat themselves. By capturing in chart form how a stock or the market is moving, a technical analyst can see the signals to buy or sell as appropriate to profit from and avoid the losses associated with price gyrations.

When this technical approach was first introduced to investment professionals and the public, many viewed it sceptically, equating it with reading tea leaves or goat entrails to predict the future. However, over time it became clear that certain human behaviours are expressed repeatedly in the financial markets. These patterns can be visually depicted and their implications revealed when price and volume data are plotted in chart format. All technical analysts have access to essentially the same information, which leads many of them to exactly the same conclusions. Therefore, if they place buy or sell orders in similar positions to take advantage of the situation, it makes the outcome look like a self-fulfilling prophecy.

The stock market indices are widely analysed as professionals look to and cite past trends and indicators for future market behaviour. For example, if a professional writes in a report that, 'After three 250-point drops, the stock market has historically surged by 7–9% in the next month', he or she is using technical analysis, in this case to reassure investors about the recovery of the market and the opportunity to profit from the short-term move.

Broad-Market Indices

The four key broad-market indices that are followed daily and used as part of technical analysis are:

- *FTSE 100.* This is the most widely published and quoted index for the UK stock market. It consists of the 100 largest UK-domiciled, blue-chip, listed and traded companies on the London Stock Exchange (LSE), using criteria established with the *Financial Times* (FT). [Note: FTSE, the group that produces various indices, was a joint venture between LSE and the FT. It is now wholly owned by the LSE.] The FTSE is a 'capitalisation-weighted index'. This means that larger companies with the most outstanding shares (not including *restricted stock* – i.e. shares issued to management that have restrictions on how long they must be held and when they can be sold) at the highest price have the greatest influence over the index. The composition of the FTSE 100 represents close to 85% of the total capitalisation of the shares on the London Stock Exchange. It is therefore a 'large-capitalisation index' and is considered a leading measure or indicator of business prosperity in the UK.

- *FTSE 250.* Also a capitalisation-weighted index, the FTSE 250 consists of the next 250 companies, by capitalisation on the London Stock Exchange that do not qualify for the FTSE 100 Index in terms of their size and liquidity. This is said to be a mid-cap index. It represents between 13% and 14% of the total capitalisation of the companies listed on the LSE. The FTSE 100 plus the FTSE 250 are referred to as the FTSE 350.

- *FTSE All-Share.* As the name denotes, this is an index of all company shares (including those in the FTSE 100 and 250 indices) that trade on the London Stock Exchange (which numbered approximately 650 in 2012). This capitalisation-weighted index is considered to be the broadest measure of the UK economy, representing 98% of total market capitalisation.

- *FTSE Small Cap.* This index represents approximately 2% of the total capitalisation of the LSE and considers those listed and traded companies that are not included in the FTSE 100 and 250 indices.

FTSE has also created narrow-based indices that capture the performance of certain sectors, such as basic industries, consumer goods, information technology and financials. Additionally, virtually all countries with stock exchanges have their own broad-based indices to track the performance of their domestic stock markets – for example, CAC 40 (France), DAX (Germany), S&P 500 (US), TSX Composite (Canada), Bovespa (Brazil), Hang Seng (Hong Kong), and Nikkei 225 (Japan). Their movements are also depicted on the different types of charts used in technical analysis.

Charts for Technical Analysis

Three types of charts are used predominantly as the fundamental tools of technical analysis. They are a *line chart*, a *bar chart*, and a *moving average chart*. In all three graphs, the price of stock or value of an index is shown on the vertical axis (the *y axis*) and time is shown on a horizontal axis (the *x axis*). Figures 4-1, 4-2 and 4-3, in the sections that follow, show the FTSE 100 index for the same period on the three kinds of charts. Notice how different the same information looks on each. Different analysts choose the charting form that provides the price sensitivity and amount of information that is needed to predict an upcoming move of the market or a particular stock.

Line Chart

This is the easiest charting method to understand and to implement. It is also the chart that investors see most often displayed on television business news programmes and financial websites throughout the trading day. As Figure 4–1 shows, the line is formed by plotting on a graph the price at which a stock was traded, or the value to which the index had risen or fallen in five- or ten-minute intervals moving from left to right. Charts covering longer periods of time, like those that show a stock's or the market's movement for a month or more, are created using the closing prices on each business day throughout the period.

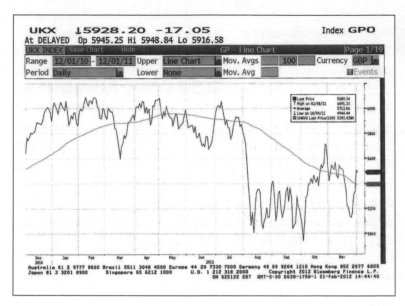

Figure 4-1: Example of a line chart showing the closing prices of the FTSE 100 from 1 December 2010 to 1 December 1 2011.

For many technical analysts this chart is too simple. It does not show, for example, the range over which the share price moved in a trading session, or whether its closing price was near the high or low point during the session.

Bar Chart
This is the chart, shown in Figure 4–2 preferred by many technical analysts because it provides more information about stock-price movement than a line chart. The price for each trading day is shown as a vertical bar. The top represents the highest value to which the stock or the index rose and the bottom represents the lowest to which it dropped. The closing

value of the security is indicated by a short horizontal line coming out of the right side of the price bar. Some bar charts also include the opening value of the stock or index as a short horizontal line coming off the left side of the vertical bar. For analysts using bar charts, it's important to know if the stock is closing consistently at the bottom or top of its daily price range because this could indicate that there is increasing momentum for a stronger move in that same direction.

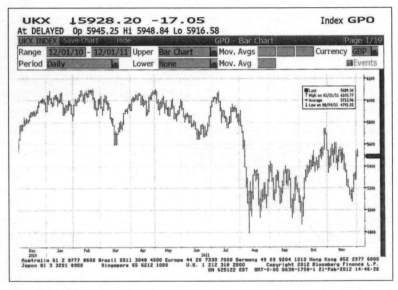

Figure 4-2: Example of a bar chart showing the movement of the FTSE 100 from 1 December 2010 to 1 December 2011.
[Each individual vertical bar shows the highest and lowest value the FTSE 100 moved to during the trading session. The small horizontal bar to the right shows the value at which the index closed.]

When using line charts and bar charts, analysts look for certain formations (head-and-shoulders top, rounded bottoms, flag, pennants, etc.) to be created by the security's price movement. They then check to see if the market strength – i.e. an increasing or decreasing number of shares being bought or sold in a given period of time or during a trading session – supports their conclusion about the impending price rise or fall. If, for example, the market is rising on increasing volume, the analyst will expect the rise to continue. On the other hand, if the market is rising on decreasing volume, an analyst may interpret this to mean that the rally is about to sputter out and will be followed by a price decline.

After years of writing about and illustrating the various technical formations, I now believe the best way to learn them and the various ways they can be interpreted is through a course with an industry practitioner or via an online course at one of the charting services. Seeing the charts and formations on a computer monitor just as a professional trader does every day makes it easier to understand the underlying concepts and how they manifest themselves dynamically in the investment markets.

Moving Average Chart

Along with bar charting, moving averages (MAs) are one of the oldest and most widely used tools of technical analysis. A moving average charts a stock's average price over a fixed, but rolling period of time (e.g. 30 days, 90 days, 100 days, or 200 days). This fixed period serves as the divisor when calculating the average. Each day the average is recomputed to include the most recent day's closing price average within the fixed period of the index, and the most distant value is dropped. This feature is why the average is described as moving. This new average amount is then recorded on the graph.

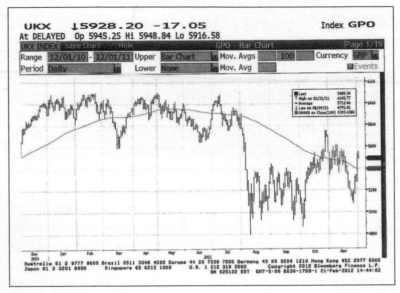

Figure 4-3: Example of a bar chart with a moving average chart. It shows the movement of the FTSE 100 from 1 December 2010 to 1 December 2011.

As the chart in Figure 4-3 shows, the moving average runs like an undulating line through the daily prices shown on the bar chart. The effect of calculating an average this way is that the daily volatility of the market is smoothed out. The longer the fixed period over which the moving average is calculated, the less sensitive the average will be to a stock's or the market's daily movement. Using a moving average therefore enables a technical analyst to stay focused on the overall trend in a stock's or the market's movement, without getting lost in the day-to-day volatility.

As with many charting methods, there are more complicated ways to construct them and various interpretations that an analyst can make. There are two classic ways in which analysts use moving averages to predict future price movement. The first compares the daily closing price movement of a stock to its moving average (100-day or 200-day) to determine if it is time to buy or sell a security. If a stock's daily closing price moves above its moving average and, at the same time, the moving average is also moving upwards, analysts interpret this as a buy signal. They expect the stock price to continue to move higher because the long-term trend, depicted by the moving average, is upward. Conversely, if a stock's daily closing price moves below its moving average and the moving average is also declining, then this is a sell signal. The price of the stock will only move lower.

The second use of this charting method is called the moving average crossover. It compares a shorter moving average (for example, a 30-day average) to a longer moving average (usually a 200-day average). When the shorter average moves above the longer average and they are both moving upward, this is thought to be a buy signal. On the other hand, a sell signal would be indicated when the shorter average moves below the longer average and they are both moving lower.

The primary advantage of using charts of moving averages to identify buy or sell signals is that you will find yourself always on the right side of the market momentum. Indeed, you will be buying when the overall price momentum for a stock is bullish or selling when the overall price momentum is bearish. The disadvantage is that you are getting into the market late. By the time the chart reveals the movement, it has already begun to happen; however, the chart does not say that continued strength or weakness is unlikely. People who use moving averages as a tool understand that it will not assist them in perfecting the timing of their trades (i.e. buying at the bottom or selling at the top). Their goal is to enter the 'belly' or middle of the trade with confidence when there is sufficient evidence that the trend has taken hold and is likely to continue for some time.

Other Technical Factors

Another group of measures often used in conjunction with charting to evaluate the market are *sentiment indicators*. They are used to determine how optimistic (bullish) or pessimistic (bearish) individual and institutional investors feel about the future direction of the overall stock market. Two easy-to-understand indicators of sentiment are the *breadth of the market* and the *trading volume*.

The *breadth of the market* is the total number of individual companies listed on a stock exchange whose shares are bought and sold on a given trading day. This number will vary from day to day and from one market to the next. Nonetheless, the greater the number of listed companies traded, the greater the breadth of the market. An analyst compares the number of issues advancing in price to those declining in price. If more companies are advancing, then the net difference when the advances and declines are subtracted from each other is positive; if more shares are declining, then the difference is negative. The net amount is then divided by the total number of listed issues that were traded that day. This result is the percentage that participated in the advance or the decline.

Increasingly positive percentages over a period indicate a technically bullish market. Investors are optimistic and are buying. More and more companies' shares are increasing in price, so the upward momentum is spreading across the stock market. Increasingly negative percentages indicate a technically bearish market – investors are becoming more cautious and pessimism is spreading. During either a bullish or bearish trend, if the net percentage slowly or suddenly shifts and begins to increase in the opposite direction, this is seen as a sign that the market is about to change direction. An investor would therefore take the appropriate buy or sell action in response to the anticipated change.

The name for the theory just discussed is the *advance-decline theory*. The positive or negative percentage that the calculation yields is called the *advance-decline ratio.* A variation on the same idea compares the number of issues reaching 52-week highs to those reaching 52-week lows. A greater percentage of issues reaching high prices indicates a bullish trend, and a higher percentage reaching low prices confirms a bearish trend. Again, a shift in the percentages after a clearly established trend would indicate an upcoming change in direction. Either the market has reached a high and is about to decline, or it has bottomed out and is about to rally.

Trading volume is always examined in conjunction with the uptrend or downtrends revealed by the ratios discussed above. High volume confirms and supports the trend. It says that more and more investors and traders are participating in the market direction. Low trading volume, on the other hand, tends to be interpreted as being inconsequential. Sudden, unexpected changes in volume should be investigated immediately. Other than calling your broker, the Internet is the fastest tool for doing this. The news may be positive, and therefore the trend is likely to continue; or negative news can prompt a wave of selling.

Summary

Today, making charts to use in technical analysis is easier, more accurate, and more efficient than ever. Virtually everyone's computer has high-tech graphic capabilities on their desktop and they are connected to the Internet via broadband data transmission. Charting services are offered by many investment websites – some for free, some by subscription only, and nearly all of these give investors the ability to create customised charts. As a result, a person using technical analysis no longer needs to rely on only one charting method; instead, he or she can use several, trying to further substantiate or confirm a signal found on one chart.

Given the easy access to up-to-the-second market data, the surge in the practice of charting (especially by day traders, high-frequency traders and hedge funds), and the high degree of exposure that technicians' interpretations get across all financial media, it is safe to say that technical analysis is today a powerful resource in assessing the markets, and the resulting technical trading will remain a powerful influence on the markets' movements.

At the very least, a light investigation of charting and sentiment indicators will perhaps help you understand some of the investment ideas discussed in the media or offered to you by your broker or financial adviser, especially those where the professional refers to a historical break in a trend, or recurring market events to support a current point of view.

Finally, you will probably want to know which is better: fundamental analysis or technical analysis? There is no simple answer to that question. It's all about what you prefer. Some investors will want to do their own detailed fundamental analysis of companies that interest them. Others will want to allow the overall markets to guide them with clues as to whether conditions are strengthening or weakening. Most of the rest of us will fall somewhere in between – using some of the core, basic principles of both approaches – if for no other reason than to gain more overall clarity about an investment, whether we already hold it or are considering buying it. While you may rely on your broker or financial adviser for ideas and guidance, or visit favourite websites for information, a foundational knowledge of both analytical methods will help you understand more clearly what an investment professional is saying when creating a plan or strategy to help you achieve your financial objectives using the stock market. This awareness will increase your comfort level with – and curiosity about – what you hear and read about the markets in all media. In turn, you will make decisions that are better informed, that are less likely to be filled with regret and more likely to be filled with the acceptance that you made a choice that was most appropriate for your individual circumstances.

5

FIXED-INCOME SECURITIES: GILTS AND CORPORATE BONDS

Bonds and other debt securities are among the various types of instruments issued by corporations and governments in order to raise capital. In fact, governments only issue debt securities. While ordinary and preference shares represent ownership in a company, bonds represent loans to the issuer. In reality, it's a debt or an IOU. The corporation, government, or other entity issuing the bond is borrowing money from the purchaser of the bond and promising that it will 1) pay interest to the bondholder at regular intervals (every six months or once a year); and 2) repay the principal or face value at maturity. These are legal obligations that are set out in the covenants (part of the bond contract) when the debt security is issued.

Unlike dividend payments on shares, interest payments are not at the discretion of a company's Board of Directors. The issuer must pay the interest when it is due. If it does not, then the issuer is in default. If a government defaults, it would most certainly be a domestic financial crisis, but also, as we have seen with the crisis in the Eurozone, this can affect other economies worldwide, depending on who holds the bonds. If a corporation defaults, it is probably heading towards being restructured or liquidated.

Bonds are a relatively straightforward investment

product or asset class. Basically, an investor knows what cash flows (interest and principal) he or she can expect with varying degrees of certainty depending on the bond's credit rating (keep in mind that an issuer's financial situation can change unexpectedly.) This sense of reasonable certainty is the appeal of bonds to people who buy them, planning to hold them to maturity. What makes bonds complicated to understand is: 1) the terminology (sometimes there are three terms all describing or denoting exactly the same thing); 2) the different features a company or entity gives its bonds to make them attractive to potential buyers or to give the issuer certain advantageous financial options in the future; and 3) the way a specific bond responds to interest-rate changes, given the financial condition of the issuer and economic environment at that time.

Bond Terminology

Principal and Coupon Rate

Corporations and governments usually try to issue each bond at a price of £100 per bond (or multiples thereof such as £1,000). Regardless of the total sterling value of the bond offering, at its most basic the issuer wants to borrow £100 from the purchaser of each bond today and, at a fixed date in the future (the bond's maturity date), repay the £100 loan. This amount that is borrowed and/ or paid at maturity has four names: *nominal value, face value, par value*, or *principal*. The price of a bond is stated as a percentage of par value (£100).

Over the bond's *term* (the number of years from the initial borrowing until the maturity date when the loan is repaid), the issuer promises to pay a fixed rate of interest at regular intervals, either every six months or once a year. This fixed annual interest rate has three names: *coupon rate* (or simply *coupon*), *nominal yield*, or *stated yield*. It is expressed as a percentage of the bond's principal value, *not* the bond's market value. (This is a common confusion.) For example, a bond with a coupon rate of 5% will pay a total of £5 [5% x £100] annually or 250p semi-annually. This amount will be paid regardless of whether the bond's current market price was above £100 (called *trading at a premium*) or below £100 (called *trading at a discount*).

The coupon rate on a bond is not set by the corporation or government that issues the debt security. In the case of corporate bonds, it is set by the investment banks hired to help price and sell the bonds to institutions and the public. In the case of gilts, it is set through an auction process in which authorised dealers bid competitively, specifying the coupon rate they would set on the bonds.

An objective of every bond issuer, whether a corporation or the government, is to keep its cost of borrowing (that is, the interest rate it will pay) as low as possible. The investment banks (also called the *underwriters*) analyse the current interest-rate environment (such as the Bank of England's base rate), the market sentiment about bonds, and the financial condition of the issuer (especially its credit risk – the possibility that the issuer will be unable to repay the loan), among other factors. An underwriter's objective is to determine what is the lowest interest rate at which they can set the bond's coupon and still be able to 1) issue the bond at £100, and 2) sell out the entire offering.

Some companies issue bonds at par value without a

fixed coupon rate. These are called *floaters*. The coupon rate is periodically reset, usually in line with changes in a benchmark interest rate such as the LIBOR (the London Interbank Offer Rate) or the Euribor (Euro Interbank Offer Rate). The bond's issuer determines the intervals (e.g. every six months, once a year) at which the coupon rate will be reset. It varies among issuers. Institutional investors like floaters, especially during a period when interest rates are expected to rise. As the benchmark rate goes up, so will the coupon rates on the floaters. The holder therefore avoids being stuck holding a portfolio of fixed-rate, low-coupon bonds when higher interest rates are prevalent in the market.

Corporations can also issue bonds that have no coupon rate. These are called *zero-coupon bonds*. 'Zeros', as they are widely known, pay no interest over their term. Instead, these bonds are issued at a discount (below the bond's principal value) and eventually mature at the principal value. The difference between the discounted issue price and the principal repaid (£100) at maturity is the interest an investor earns on a zero-coupon bond. As long as an investor holds a zero to maturity and the issuer does not default, he or she will get the promised interest rate.

While a corporation that issues zero-coupon bonds does not have to pay interest over the term of the bond, it does have to put money aside to repay the nominal value at maturity. Most corporate zeros have what is known as a *sinking fund provision*. This means that the issuer must deposit money into an escrow account at regular intervals so that it accumulates the money needed to redeem the bonds at maturity. The account is called an escrow account because it is held by a third party, usually a bank or trustee, which safeguards the money for the bondholders.

I have been very careful here to say that corporations issue zero-coupon bonds. Governments typically cannot. In order to maintain a top-tier credit rating (discussed later in this chapter), a government must demonstrate its ability to make interest payments on time. Government-backed zero-coupons are created by authorised dealers through a complex process known as *stripping*. In simple terms, interest payments and the principal repayment on a normal coupon bond are each treated as a separate stream of money (also called a *cash flow*) and regarded as an individual security. A ten-year, fixed-rate coupon bond, for example, becomes 21 separate zeros – one for each of the 20 six-month interest payments over the ten-year term and one for the principal repayment at maturity.

Zero-coupon bonds were originally created with the small investor in mind. Because the bonds are issued at a discount (below £100), a small investor could more easily afford to buy them. Equally important, the investor would know exactly how much money he or she would receive when each bond matures at £100.

When interest rates are high, long-term zeros are issued at a deep discount. During times when interest rates are low, the discount is small, and therefore less attractive. Overall, zero-coupon bonds can be effectively used to accumulate a specific amount of money by a targeted date, such as on retirement or when a child's university fees must be paid.

Yield

Perhaps the most important word to understand in the bond markets is 'yield'. It's also one of the most confusing because there are so many different types of yields. One has already been discussed in the section on Principal and Coupon Rate: a bond's nominal yield or stated yield. This is the annual percentage of the bond's interest payment. It is what most retail investors mean when we use the term *yield*. We want to know how much interest income we will be paid on the bond every six months or once a year. And we expect that the principal will be repaid at maturity.

Investors sometimes also focus on *current yield* when they buy bonds in the secondary market. Also referred to as the *income yield* or *running yield*, it is calculated by dividing a bond's annual coupon payment by the market price at which the bond is trading.

$$\text{Current Yield} = \left(\frac{\text{Annual Interest Amount}}{\text{Bond's Current Market Price}} \right) \times 100$$

To illustrate this, let's say an investor is interested in a bond with a 5% coupon. He purchases the bond when it's trading in the secondary marketplace at a discounted price of £90. The bond's current yield is 5.56% [£5 ÷ £90]. If a bond by another issuer has a 5% coupon but is trading at a premium of £110, then that bond would have a current yield of 4.55% [£5 ÷ £110].

As these two examples show, current yield is a simple snapshot of the value of the coupon relative to the price you're paying for the bond. If an investor buys a bond at a discount, then the interest payments offer a current or income yield that is higher than the bond's coupon rate. If the bond is bought at a premium, then the interest provides a current or income yield that is lower than the bond's coupon. And if the bond is bought at par value, then the current yield and the coupon rate will be the same. [Note: The current yield formula for a bond or other fixed income security is the same as the dividend yield formula for a share.]

Financial service professionals, however, use the word *yield* to mean *yield to maturity* (YTM). In the UK this is also referred to as the *yield to redemption* (YTR), the *gross redemption yield* (GRY) and gross redemption. When an article in the FT notes that Greece's ten-year bonds yield 15% in the secondary market and its two-year bonds yield over 20%, the writer is talking about the bond's yield to maturity, not its coupon rate or current yield.

YTR is a complex calculation. In addition to considering the amount of each coupon payment, and the time at which each is made over the bond's term, the formula takes into account two additional cash flows on a bond: 1) the interest earned on the coupon payments if they were immediately reinvested; and 2) the gain that would be made over the life of the bond if it were bought at a discount (or the loss over the bond's life if it were bought at a premium).

It's not necessary to do the calculation to understand the concept underlying YTR. (If you are curious about the actual formula, there are many financial websites that explain it in detail, as well as show how to do the calculation.) However, there are two assumptions built into the formula that are important to keep in mind. First, the calculation assumes the bond will be held to maturity and that it will be redeemed at the principal value. If you sell before it reaches maturity, then you will most likely realise either a gain or a loss; therefore, the total return you realise will either be higher or lower, respectively, than the YTR. Secondly, the formula assumes the bondholder immediately reinvests each semi-annual or annual coupon payment at the bond's YTR rate – not its coupon rate. The YTR rate is assumed because each coupon payment will, in turn, earn interest (i.e. interest on interest) until the bond matures. In reality, the rate at which each coupon payment can be reinvested, if they are, will vary. As well, for the majority of bondholders, the assumption that they will not spend the interest payments is unrealistic.

So what is the benefit of having a basic understanding of YTR, and how is it used by industry professionals? For the retail investor, understanding the terminology helps you to better evaluate the difference between, for example, a bond with a high yield to maturity and one with a high coupon rate. What do the different rates indicate about the cash flows from the bonds as well as the risks associated with each? For professionals, using YTR helps them more accurately compare bonds that have different coupons and are trading in the market at different prices. Perhaps most importantly, understanding YTR makes it clear why bond prices move opposite to interest rate changes, and how a rising or falling bond price directly affects the YTR movement in the trading markets.

The relationship between a bond's secondary market price, its coupon rate and its yield to maturity can be summarised in three statements that can serve as useful basic guidelines.

1. If a bond's YTR is greater than its coupon rate, then the bond is trading at a discount – i.e. below par value. The higher the YTR (as was the case with the Greek government bond in 2011 and 2012), then the lower or more discounted the market price will be.

2. If a bond's YTR is lower than its coupon rate, then the bond is trading at a premium – i.e. above par value. Because the bond is purchased above par value, there will be a loss when the bond matures at par value. This loss reduces the total return received from the bond's interest payment. Therefore, the lower the YTR, the higher the premium price of the bond will be.
3. If a bond's YTR equals its coupon rate, then the bond is trading at par value.

One question invariably arises during a discussion of YTR: why would anyone buy a bond that is trading at a premium, knowing they will have a loss if they hold the bond to its maturity? The reason is the bond's coupon rate. If a bond is trading at the premium, it means that the yield has gone down. [Remember: as yield goes down, bond prices rise.] A bond with a coupon rate that is higher than yield on bonds currently available in the market will be very attractive to investors. They are willing to pay the premium price so that they can get the higher interest payments. In short, receiving the higher interest income now (perhaps to use for living expenses) is more important to the investor than the small amount they will lose on the bond's nominal value in the distant future.

At many trading desks around the world the term *basis* is used as in, 'The 4% bond is selling at a 4.75% basis.' In this statement, 4% refers to the bond's coupon rate and 4.75% is the yield to redemption or to maturity. An investor would accurately conclude that this bond is selling at a discount in the secondary market, because the YTR is higher than the bond's coupon rate.

The term *basis point* is a widely used term related

to basis that an investor in bonds and gilts needs to understand. It is abbreviated as 'bps' (basis points) and pronounced 'bips' (rhyming with lips). A basis point is the smallest increment for quoting the yield on a bond. It is 0.01% of a yield to redemption quote. If a bond's yield to redemption changes from 4.75% to 4.95%, that is a change of 0.20% [4.95% minus 4.75%] or a change of 20 basis points. Understanding bps can provide an investor with a quick reference point to understanding certain costs related to bonds.

If one basis point, 0.01%, is translated into a pound amount for a bond with a £100 par value or nominal value, every basis point has a value of 1p [£100 x 0.0001]. If the bond has a par value of £100, then every basis point has a value of 10p [£1000 x 0.0001]. These values serve as useful reference points. If you hear that a corporate bond is trading 25 bps over a comparable gilt, you'll know that the YTR is approximately 0.25% higher; therefore, the price of the corporate bond would be approximately 25p cheaper (for every £100 par value of the bond) than the market price of the comparable gilt. This is an approximation because other factors, such as the bond's rating, coupon rate, and length of time to maturity, affect the actual price at which the bond is trading in the secondary market.

And finally, bps are also used to quantify the amount of compensation, ongoing or one-off, that a brokerage firm or other financial institution receives. Let's say that a brokerage firm receives trailing commissions (those paid for as long as the individual's money remains invested in the products) of 50 bps annually. This means that for every £1,000 the investor has invested, the brokerage firm will receive £5 as annual compensation.

If, for example, you have £100,000 invested in a fund, the company who advised you to buy it would receive £500 per year. Understanding the fundamentals of basis points (bps) enables an investor to have a clearer understanding of YTR in the fixed income markets and compensation on other types of investments.

Bond Covenants or Features

When issuing a new corporate bond, a company will sometimes add features that 1) give it flexibility to redeem the bond early if interest rates decline; and 2) make the bond attractive to potential purchasers. The specific features added depend on the conditions in the investment markets at the time the bonds are issued, as well as what the issuer believes will help make the offering successful. Two of the most common features are *callable bonds* and *puttable bonds*.

Callable Bond

A call feature on a bond, if it exists, gives the company the right to buy back the bond from the bondholder before its maturity. In short, the company can redeem the bond early. A company is likely to exercise the call feature when interest rates in the marketplace have dropped substantially (a relative term) below the bond's coupon rate. Where does the company get the money to pay for the bond it calls? Typically, it first issues a new bond with a low coupon rate (remember, interest rates have dropped) and then uses the money raised from the new issuance to call an older bond that has a higher coupon rate. The process is called *refunding*. It is very similar to what people do when they refinance their homes to lower mortgage rates.

The details of the call are stated when the bond is issued. Typically, they specify the periods when the issuer can begin calling the bond and the price at which it can do so. The call price (also referred to as the redemption price) may be predetermined (such as at par value) or based on a formula relating to a gilt yield, for example. The price also depends generally on whether the call is 'partial' or 'in-whole'. (Virtually all companies give themselves both options, stating in the call covenant that the bond is callable 'in part or in whole'.) In a partial call, the specific bonds within an outstanding issue are called at random. The investors whose bonds are chosen may receive a slight premium (above par value) as small compensation for the future interest payments they will not receive. An in-whole call means the company can redeem the entire bond issue at one time. Since all bondholders are being equally inconvenienced, the issuer usually pays only par value when the bonds are called.

Companies take this action to reduce the amount of interest they will have to pay over the long-term. All calls are mandatory. On a set day the bond will stop paying interest and any premium call price being offered will expire. The bond will then be redeemable only at par value.

When there is reasonable certainty in the market that a bond will be called, its price is no longer quoted on a yield-to-redemption basis. Instead, *yield to call* (YTC) is used. The call date becomes the *de facto* new maturity date. Since the call date is shorter than the original maturity date, the bond will earn fewer coupon payments and the theoretically reinvested payments will earn less interest on interest. Hence, the YTC may be lower than the YTR.

Puttable Bonds

A bond with the put feature gives the bondholder the right to tender (sell) the bond back to the corporation, usually at par value. A customer is likely to exercise the put when interest rates are rising. The investor wants to get back the bond's par value so that he or she can reinvest the money in other securities that offer a higher coupon rate or yield to redemption. The periods during which the bonds can be put back (i.e. tendered), as well as the total face amount of bonds that the issuer will buy back during each period, are stated in the bond's covenants when it is first issued. Bonds with a put feature tend to pay a lower coupon rate. The put option may also be linked to a change in control or change in the business that relates in a downgrade in the bond's credit rating.

The call and put features discussed above can be found on corporate bonds. While some older types of gilts are callable, it's not typical for governments to issue bonds with call or put features. The features that a specific bond issue has can be obtained from the bond's initial offering document, from your stockbroker or financial adviser, from the stock exchange, or from any third party vendor offering information about fixed income securities. It is important to know what features a bond has because these can affect the return that you, the investor, may or may not receive.

Gilts

Gilts are debt obligations of the government of the United Kingdom and are issued by HM Treasury. The Debt Management Office (DMO) manages the Gilt market on behalf of the Treasury. The primary dealers in UK government debt are called Gilt Edge Market Makers (GEMMs) and they essentially control the market by buying and selling convention and/or index-linked gilts in the trading markets everyday. Before April 2005, the debt securities were referred to as *Treasury Stock*. All UK government bonds issued after that date are referred to as *Treasury Gilts*. [Note: The still widely used phrase 'stocks and shares' came about during the days when bonds were referred to as 'stock'. Today, since the words 'stock' and 'shares' are synonyms in most investment markets around the world, the continued use of the old-fashioned phrase can be confusing. Furthermore, the UK government refers to interest payments on its index-link gilts, for example, as dividend payments, a term commonly used for periodic payments received on equity securities. This only adds to investors' sense that learning about the stock market is like learning a foreign language.]

Like equities, gilts trade on the London Stock Exchange. The name, a shortening of the phrase 'gilt edge', comes from the fact that these securities are viewed as among the safest in the world. The UK government has never defaulted on the interest payments on the gilts it has issued or on the principal repayments when the gilts mature. Its debt, therefore, has the highest rating for safety.

Today the UK government issues two kinds of gilts:

conventional and *index-linked*. There are also older types, like *undated gilts* and war loans that still trade on the stock exchange and are included in the financial media's reporting of trading activity (see Figure 5.1 below).

GILTS - UK CASH MARKET   www.ft.com/gilts

Dec 30	Notes	Price £	day's Chng	wk% Chng	Red Yield	52 Week High	Low
Shorts (Lives up to Five Years)							
Tr 7.75pc '12-15♦		100.46	-0.08	-0.2	0.38	107.28	100.36
Tr 5pc '12		100.84	-0.05	-0.1	0.22	105.05	100.80
Tr 5.25pc '12		102.11	-0.06	-0.1	0.29	106.34	102.06
Tr 9pc '12	♦	105.10	-0.09	-0.2	0.37	112.94	104.76
Tr 8pc '13		113.23	-0.12	-0.2	0.33	118.32	113.12
Tr 4.5pc '13		104.92	-0.06	-0.1	0.31	107.32	104.84
Tr 2.25pc '14		104.18	-0.08	0.0	0.32	104.36	100.40
Tr 5pc '14		112.33	-0.10	-0.1	0.37	112.97	109.05
Tr 2.75pc '15		106.88	-0.08	0.1	0.48	107.08	100.68
Tr 4.75pc '15		115.16	-0.13	0.0	0.58	115.62	108.49
Tr 8pc '15		128.52	-0.18	0.0	0.63	129.42	123.34
Tr 2pc '16		104.96	-0.08	0.2	0.76	105.22	95.68
Tr 4pc '16		114.29	-0.11	0.2	0.87	114.96	104.77
Five to Ten Years							
Tr 1.75pc '17		103.46	-0.09	0.2	1.05	103.78	99.98
Tr 3.75pc '21		115.57	-0.14	0.5	1.97	116.07	98.17
Tr 8.75pc '17		141.85	-0.17	0.1	1.09	142.32	132.55
Tr 5pc '18		122.22	-0.13	0.2	1.25	122.52	109.57
Tr 3.75pc '19		115.31	-0.13	0.4	1.62	115.67	99.24
Tr 4.5pc '19		120.44	-0.13	0.3	1.49	120.76	105.22
Tr 3.75pc '20		115.62	-0.15	0.5	1.80	115.99	98.01
Tr 4.75pc '20		123.34	-0.15	0.4	1.68	123.72	106.39
Tr 8pc '21		153.13	-0.22	0.4	1.84	153.63	133.53

Notes	Price £	day's Chng	wk% Chng	Red Yield	52 Week High	Low
Ten to Fifteen Years						
Tr 5pc '25	130.34	-0.21	0.6	2.32	130.88	107.23
Over Fifteen Years						
Tr 4.25pc '27	122.19	-0.33	0.7	2.55	122.93	97.65
Tr 6pc '28	147.27	-0.41	0.7	2.55	148.17	119.26
Tr 4.75pc '30	129.45	-0.44	0.7	2.74	130.40	102.70
Tr 4.25pc '32	121.96	-0.44	0.8	2.83	122.90	95.76
Tr 4.5pc '34	126.26	-0.50	0.8	2.91	127.30	98.36
Tr 4.25pc '36	122.58	-0.54	0.8	2.94	123.74	94.77
Tr 4.75pc '38	132.64	-0.60	0.9	2.98	133.92	102.64
Tr 4.25pc '40	122.92	-0.60	0.9	3.05	124.50	94.20
Tr 4.5pc '42	128.86	-0.66	0.9	3.05	130.89	98.63
Tr 4.25pc '46	125.26	-0.69	1.0	3.07	127.85	94.67
Tr 4.25pc '49	126.33	-0.71	1.0	3.07	129.23	94.85
Tr 3.75pc '52	115.15	-0.68	1.1	3.09	117.90	100.15
Tr 4.25pc '55	128.59	-0.80	1.1	3.06	131.92	95.27
Tr 4pc '60	123.78	-0.82	1.2	3.05	126.98	90.13
Undated						
Cons 4pc ♦	100.42	-0.03	0.0	3.98‡	102.53	75.82
War Ln 3.5pc	97.18	-1.09	0.4	3.60‡	99.18	71.49
Ch 3.5 pc '61 Aft ♦	94.39	-0.93	0.4	3.71‡	98.72	69.92
Tr 3pc '66 Aft ♦	78.99	-0.76	0.4	3.80‡	80.50	58.87
Cons 2.5pc ♦	67.98	-0.67	0.5	3.68‡	69.28	50.25
Tr 2.5pc ♦	69.48	-0.71	0.5	3.60‡	70.98	51.06

Notes	Price £	day's Chng	Yld (1)	(2)	52 Week High	Low
Index-linked						
2.5pc '13	(82) 283.45	-0.14	-0.1 -2.79	-2.17	287.78	277.22
2.5pc '16	(L) 341.39	-0.33	0.1 -1.58	-1.33	343.78	309.72
1.25pc '17	(78) 115.34	-0.14	0.1 -1.06	-1.06	115.84	106.40
2.5pc '20	(83) 363.92	-0.68	0.2 -0.73	-0.59	365.50	312.91
1.875pc '22	(350) 127.58	-0.31	0.3 -0.30	-0.30	228.60	110.93
2.5pc '24	(97) 331.09	-0.76	0.4 -0.26	-0.17	333.01	274.72
1.25pc '27†	(349) 125.27	-0.52	0.4 -0.10	-0.10	126.33	104.22
0.125pc '29	105.74	-0.55	0.4 -0.17	-0.11	106.08	100.14
4.125pc '30	(35) 319.19	-1.50	0.3 -0.17	-0.09	322.21	260.91
2pc '35	(78) 204.59	-1.47	0.3 -0.09	-0.03	207.23	159.86
1.25pc '32†	(328) 131.04	-0.83	0.3 -0.03	-0.03	132.60	105.94
0.75pc '34	(288) 120.16	-0.84	0.3 0.01	0.03	120.69	104.53
1.125pc '37†	(348) 133.97	-1.17	0.2 -0.03	-0.03	135.90	105.31
0.625pc '40†	(319) 121.63	-1.19	0.3 -0.02	-0.02	123.77	93.15
0.625pc '42†	(327) 123.94	-1.23	0.4 -0.04	-0.04	125.49	93.56
0.75pc '47†	(307) 131.68	-1.67	0.2 -0.04	-0.04	134.90	98.03
0.5pc '50	(298) 123.89	-1.63	0.3 -0.04	-0.04	124.99	90.52
1.25pc '55†	(300) 161.42	-2.15	0.3 -0.05	-0.05	166.16	120.48
0.375pc '62	125.35	-2.26	0.2 -0.05	-0.05	127.61	99.72

Prospective real redemption rate on projected inflation of (1) 5% and (2) 3%.
(b) Figures in parentheses show RPI base for indexing (8 months prior to issue and (for gilts issued since September 2005, 3 months prior to issue) and have been adjusted to reflect rebasing of RPI to 100 in January 1987. Conversion factor 3.945. RPI for Sep 2009: 215.3 and for Apr 2009 211.5. † For those bonds indexed, with a 3m lag, the 'clean' price shown has no inflation adjustment. The yield is calculated using no inflation assumption. ‡ Running yield.

All UK Gilts are Tax free to non-residents on application. xd Ex dividend. Closing mid-prices are shown in pounds per £100 nominal of stock. Weekly percentage changes are calculated on a Friday to Friday basis. Gilt benchmarks and most liquid stocks, are shown in bold type. A full list of Gilts can be found daily on ft.com/bond&rates.   Source: ThomsonReuters

Figure 5-1: Daily column from the *Financial Times* showing the trading activity of Treasury Gilts. Notice the listing divides gilts into four groups according to maturity: up to five years to maturity (called *shorts*); five to ten years to maturity; ten to fifteen years to maturity; and over fifteen years. Index-linked gilts, the second largest type issued, are listed separately, as are older undated gilts.

Conventional Gilts

These government-backed debt securities are a regular bond, with up to 50 years to maturity. They are issued with a stated coupon rate and maturity date. In the FT listing in Figure 5-1 above, you can see 'Tr 8.75pc'17' (in the first column, under Five to Ten Years and highlighted in bold because it was among the most liquid on the trading day reported in the column). This listing denotes a Treasury Gilt with an 8.75% coupon, maturing in 2017. Conventional gilts pay interest every six months. Using this example, if an investor owns gilts with a principal value of £100, he would receive semi-annual interest payments of £4.375. If the gilts have a principal value of £1,000, the bondholder would receive £43.75 every six months. At maturity the investor receives a six-month final interest payment and the return of the bond's principal.

As you peruse the information reported in Figure 5.1, you'll notice that the different gilt issues have different coupon rates. Each reflects the prevailing interest-rate environment when the government issued the gilts. In normal times, short-term interest rates are used to manage the UK economy. Low interest rates serve to stimulate the economy because they make borrowing more attractive, while high rates cool or slow down the economy. Long-term interest rates on gilts reflect the markets' view of inflation in the future. They are the rates, at different times, that investors want in order to be compensated for its negative effect on their money. In short, fear of inflation drives long-term gilt interest rates higher. As this fear subsides, rates decline.

As shown in Figure 5.1, the prices of gilts are quoted in pounds and pence, with the minimum price fluctuation being one penny. So, the closing mid price (the midpoint between the highest bid and the lowest offer) for the Tr 8.75pc'17 bond is £141.85. This bond is trading at a substantial premium to its principal value. An investor can quickly conclude that interest rates in the broader market have declined (and subsequently bond prices have risen) since the bond was issued. An investor also knows that the redemption yield on the bond will be quite a bit less than the bond's 8.75% coupon rate.

Index-Linked Gilts

These government bonds are designed to help protect against the risk of inflation. (This is discussed in the *Risks and Rewards* section of this chapter.) The coupon rate and the principal amounts on these bonds are periodically adjusted based on the movement of the General Index of Retail Prices, which is frequently referred to as the *Retail Prices Index* (RPI). This means that in an inflationary environment the amount of interest paid to the bondholder increases at every adjustment period. Thus, in theory, the buying power of your money effectively keeps pace with inflation – i.e. the increase in the cost of goods and services. Because these gilts offer this inflation-protection feature, they are issued with a coupon rate that is lower than that of conventional gilts issued at the same time.

The calculation of the new coupon payment and the adjustment in the principal is done three months after the publication of the RPI. (In the past there was an eight-month lag, but that was changed to the shorter time in 2005.) At maturity, the bondholder receives the greater of par value or the inflation-adjusted principal amount.

More information about specific index-linked gilts can be found at the website of the UK Debt Management Office (DMO): http://www.dmo.gov.uk/index.aspx?page=About/About_Gilts.

Undated Gilts

These bonds have no fixed maturity date. Instead, they are redeemable at the discretion of the British government. They are listed separately in Figure 5.1 and include a War Loan Gilt. These debt securities were originally issued to raise money for the war in the early part of the last century. Because many of these bonds have been in the markets for decades, have historically low coupon rates, and have such a small total number of bonds outstanding and traded daily (especially compared to conventional and index-linked gilts), the government seems to have little interest in exercising its right to redeem these securities.

Stripped Gilts

These are the zero-coupon bonds that are created by dealers authorised by HM Treasury to take designated gilt issues and then separate (strip) each interest payment and the principal repayment on a bond into separate securities. Each security, backed by either one of the six-month interest payments or the repayment of principal, is issued at a discount to its principal amount. There are no interest payments over the term of a stripped gilt. Like all zeros, the investor's return is the difference between the gilt's discounted issue or purchase price and its redemption price (the principal or par value) at maturity. (See the discussion of zero-coupon bonds earlier in this chapter.)

Gilts are viewed as low-risk securities. They are not risk-free, as many people think. Even bonds issued by the safest issuer in the world are subject to interest-rate risk – the inverse movement of bond prices as a reaction to an increase or decrease in interest rates.

Corporate Bonds

Debt securities issued by companies are known as *corporate bonds* and *notes*. Like gilts, these securities have a par value of £100 and pay interest semi-annually or annually. However, they offer a higher coupon rate because they are more risky than government bonds. During periods when interest rates are low, investors will often look at high-grade corporate bonds as a way of getting a better return on their investment without substantially increasing investment risk.

Corporate debt securities are issued in a different way from equity securities (ordinary and preference shares). Companies issue bonds as part of a programme, the most common being the Euro Medium Term Note Programme. This allows a corporation to issue bonds up to a specified total nominal (principal) amount across country borders in a number of different currencies (sterling, euros, Swiss francs, etc.). Importantly, not all of the bonds issued under the programme have to be the same type. The underwriter or investment banker can give the bonds different characteristics to meet the needs of the different markets in which the corporation's debt security will be sold. [Remember: it is the investment bank that sets the coupon rate on a bond, not the issuer.]

Because each country has its own financial industry regulatory authority, cross-border issuance clearly presents a problem. Also, different types of bonds necessitate that different information be disclosed. The conflicts underlying this situation were resolved in 2005 with the implementation of the Prospectus Directive (PD) in the EU. This regulation details the standards or conditions that all new securities issuances must meet to allow for the 'passporting' of approved prospectuses throughout the EU. In bond offerings, one of the specific conditions in the Prospectus Directive is that the minimum denomination per unit must be at least €50,000. This minimum amount is likely to increase to

€100,000 in the future. Ultimately, this shows that the directive caters entirely to the traditional institutional bond investors. Bonds can be offered to retail investors but the prospectus requirements are more onerous. (A recently developed issuing and trading platform for retail investors in the UK, called the *Order Book for Retail Bonds* or *ORB*, is discussed at the end of this chapter.)

Types of Corporate Bonds

As noted at the beginning of this chapter, bonds are given various features to make them more attractive to the purchaser and to give the issuing corporation some flexibility as economic and interest-rate conditions change in the future. So, a discussion of the 'types' of corporate bonds is in reality an examination of the features that they are given when they are issued. Regardless of the type of bond, the issuer's credit rating is essential to assessing the company's ability to make its interest payments and eventually repay the principal. In fact, it is virtually impossible for a corporation to issue an unrated bond. Before it issues a bond, the company hires at least one of the rating agencies – Moody's, Standard & Poor's, and Fitch – to independently assess its creditworthiness and risk of default. (Ratings are discussed on page 136 and 137.)

Here are some (not all) of the bond types an investor interested in corporate bonds is likely to encounter.

- *Secured bond.* This bond is backed by specific assets of a company, such as its real estate, land, or the securities (equity or debt) that it holds in another corporation. If the company goes bankrupt, the secured bondholder's claim will be paid from the liquidation of the specific asset.
- *Unsecured bond.* This bond is backed by the good

faith and creditworthiness of the issuing corporation. Basically, it is the company's reputation, rather than a specific asset, that backs this bond. This is the type of bond issued most often by well-known, blue-chip companies. (Note: In the US an unsecured corporate bond is called a *debenture*. In the UK, a *debenture* is usually a secured bond.)

- *Senior bond*. This bond has first claim, among all other bondholders, on the company's assets, should the company go into liquidation.
- *Subordinated bond*. Among all other bondholders, these debt securities have the lowest priority in a claim on a company's assets in a liquidation. In fact, their claim ranks just above that of general creditors (i.e. vendors who provide services to the company).
- *Junk bond*. This description can apply to a senior, unsecured, subordinated or any other type of corporate bond. The term reflects the bond's credit rating. Junk bonds are highly speculative corporate bonds rated BB (by Standard & Poor's & Fitch), Ba (by Moody's) or lower. Junk bonds offer investors a high coupon rate to compensate them for the risk that the issuer may default on interest payments and eventual repayment of principal. [Note: A junk bond and a zero-coupon bond are not the same. The former is based on the bond's ratings, while the latter indicates that the bond makes no interest payments over its term. Zero-coupon bonds can be issued by companies with investment-grade ratings.]
- *Convertible bond*. This corporate bond gives the holder the right to convert the bond into a fixed number of ordinary shares of the same company at the specific price (called the *conversion price*). All of the terms of conversion are set when the company issues the bonds.

A bondholder is most likely to convert when the market price of the underlying ordinary shares rises significantly above its fixed conversion price. This feature lets the bondholder turn the debt security into the company's ordinary shares and thus participate in the company's capital appreciation of its share price if it rises significantly. If, however, the share price languishes at or below the conversion price, the bondholder won't convert, but will continue to receive regular interest payments (albeit at a very low coupon rate) for the term of the bond. A convertible corporate bond is frequently described as a *hybrid security* because it has characteristics of both debt securities and ordinary shares.

Other Types Of Bonds

Many people are aware of other types of bonds, other than gilts and corporate bonds, which are more widely available to – and used by – retail investors. These investment products are created by insurance companies and other financial firms and they promise to pay a fixed rate of return. In reality, they are not like the traditional bonds that trade on the stock exchange, although they use the name. The products are not tradable – that is, they cannot be bought and sold freely on a registered exchange. Instead, they are redeemable – i.e. can only be bought from or sold back to the specific insurance or financial company that created the bond. Below is a description of those bonds most widely used by the investors like you and me.

• *Guaranteed bonds.* These are issued by insurance companies and available in two types: *income bonds* and *growth bonds*. An income bond pays interest periodically (usually either monthly or annually), and at maturity the initial amount you invested is repaid to you. A growth bond pays you accumulated interest, together with the original investment, in a lump sum at maturity. With either type of guaranteed bond, the holder's heirs receive a payout if he or she dies before the maturity date. Guaranteed bonds are designed to be held to their maturity date. If the holder needs to cash in the bond before its maturity date, or if the bond doesn't generate enough income to pay the amount that's been 'guaranteed', then he or she may receive less than the original amount invested.

- *Guaranteed-equity bonds.* Typically offered by large banking institutions, these bonds are linked to a specified stock index (e.g. the FTSE 100 or the FTSE All-Share Index). They let the bondholder participate in the growth of that index over a specified period of time. If the index increases in value, so will the value of the bond. If the index declines, the bondholder is guaranteed to get his or her original investment back at maturity. Importantly, no interest is paid over the life of the bond. Therefore, guaranteed-equity bonds are not appropriate for an investor who wants to generate income. These bonds would be more suitable for an investor who has a longer-term, bullish view of the stock market and can leave their money invested, typically for five years or more. While these securities were referred to as bonds when they were originally created, they are more widely referred to as Structured Products today and are mostly issued by banks.

- *With-profits bonds.* These bonds are a life-assurance-based investment that can be purchased with a single lump-sum payment. The lump sum is invested in a professionally managed with-profits fund. (So this product is not really a 'bond'; instead, it is ownership in an underlying portfolio of securities.) The assets in the fund can include shares, bonds, cash and even property. With-profits bonds have no fixed term because the underlying portfolio has no fixed life. The holder's return from the with-profits fund includes an annual bonus and, if appropriate, a terminal bonus when the policy is cashed in. Both bonuses depend on the fund manager's success in generating profits through the investments he or she makes with the money in the fund. The holder can cash in the bond at any time he or she wishes. However, surrender penalties (also called market value reduction) may be imposed on the with-profits bond. These penalties reduce the amount of the total return the bondholder receives from the with-profits fund. The amount of life cover that comes with the purchase of the bond is minimal, usually 101% of the market value of the bond at the time of death and it is only payable if the investor dies while holding the investment.

Risks Of Investing In Bonds

There are seven basic risks that anyone interested in investing in bonds needs to understand. These are present for investors who plan to hold the bonds to maturity as well as for those who want to trade bonds.

Credit Risk
Also called *default risk*, this is the likelihood that the issuer of the bonds will not be able to make the promised

periodic interest payments over the term of the bond and
the eventual repayment of the bond's nominal or face value
at maturity. Three ratings agencies – Moody's, Standard &
Poor's, and Fitch – provide letter ratings for bonds indicating
the creditworthiness of the issuer. Looked at from a different
point of view, these ratings assess the potential for default.
Companies hire and pay for these ratings agencies (at least
one of them, sometimes all three) to evaluate a bond before
it is issued. Figure 5-2 shows the bond ratings.

CREDIT QUALITY	MOODY'S*	STANDARD & POOR'S**	FITCH'S**
Highest quality (highest ability to repay debt and least likely to default)	Aaa	AAA	AAA
High quality (very strong ability to pay interest and repay principal)	Aa	AA	AA
Upper medium grade (adequate ability to repay debt)	A	A	A
Medium grade ability to repay (lowest investment grade)	Baa	BBB	BBB
Lower medium grade (first rating that is not investment grade, indicating significant speculative elements)	Ba	BB	BB
Low grade (not a desirable investment)	B	B	B
Poor quality (may default)	Caa	CCC	CCC
Highly speculative (default is reasonably certain)	Ca	CC	CC

Lowest rating	C	C	C
(Interest payments have stopped or issuer has filed for bankruptcy)			
In default	C	D	D

* Moody's refines its tiers ratings from Aa to Ca by adding 1, 2 or 3 (e.g., A1 or BBB3) to show the bond's relative standing within the tier.
** S&P's and Fitch refine their ratings by adding plus or minus signs from tier AA to CC (e.g., A+ or BBB-) to show the bond's relative standing within a tier.

Figure 5-2: Bond Ratings by Moody's, Standard & Poor's & Fitch's. The companies rate the likelihood that the issuer will default on its interest payment and the eventual repayments of principal bonds rated Ba-BB or lower are called junk bonds.

The first four ratings (in the shaded area) are investment grade, indicating the least likelihood of default. Gilts are rated triple-A because the British government has not and probably will never default on its interest payments. [Note: During the time I was writing this book, Moody's and Standard & Poor's and Fitch warned that the United States government, the largest issuer of debt in the world, risked losing its coveted triple-A rating because of the huge amount of debt it was issuing and the political impasse in Congress about raising the US debt ceiling. Standard & Poor's downgraded US government debt to AA+, while Moody's and Fitch let its rating remain at AAA.]

The first rating at which a bond is said to have significant speculative elements is Ba (Moody's) and BB (S&P's and Fitch). Bonds with this or lower ratings are known as junk bonds. They are also called *high-yield bonds*, which the industry views as a more marketing-friendly term. Other synonyms include *sub-investment grade* and *non-investment grade*.

The lower the rating, the more interest the corporation or government (Greece, for example) must pay investors to buy the bonds to compensate for the associated risk. All of the agencies periodically review the financial condition of the issuer to determine if the rating should stay the same or change. Any change or anticipated change is announced in the financial press or on the rating agencies' websites. A downgrade is what every issuer and investor fears. If this happens, many investors may sell the bonds. This selling drives the bond's price lower. Some investors might even sell at a loss, fearful that the price may go even lower, especially if there are few buyers for the downgraded bond. It's important, even for the 'buy-and-hold' investor, to understand that the ratings can and do change. A lowered rating, for example, indicates that the risk associated with the bond has increased since it was initially purchased. Conversely, an improved rating indicates greater safety.

Interest-Rate Risk

This is the risk resulting from changes in interest rates in the overall market. Bond prices move opposite to changes in interest rates. If interest rates rise, bond prices will decline because the lower coupon rate on the bond will be less attractive to investors. Additionally, for an investor purchasing this already outstanding bond, the combination of the lower market price and the coupon rate should provide a yield to redemption that is closer to the higher rate. If interest rates decline, then bond prices will rise. This happens because more people will want to buy the older bond with the higher interest rate. The additional demand for the bond drives the price up and the bond will most likely trade above its nominal value – i.e. at a premium.

The amount by which interest-rate risk affects a bond depends on 1) its length of time to maturity; 2) its coupon rate; and 3) its credit rating. The prices of bonds with longer maturities will change more in response to changes in interest rates when compared to bonds with shorter maturities, which will respond less. As a visual representation of this price movement, imagine the fulcrum and plane that we learned about in school. The greater movement of the plane is always at the point furthest away from the fulcrum; the smaller movement is nearer the fulcrum. With this image in your mind, you should clearly be able to see that long-term bonds will always be more volatile than short-term bonds.

Bonds with lower coupons will always be more volatile (i.e. move in price more) than bonds with higher coupons, if they have the same risk profile. Imagine that you have a bond with a 5% coupon and one with an 8% coupon. If interest rates rise to 6%, people holding the bond paying 5% annual interest will probably want to sell it (thus driving the price down), whereas investors with the higher coupon are more likely to still hold the bond in their portfolios.

And finally, bonds with greater credit risk (junk bonds) are much more volatile than investment-grade bonds. Investors are likely to see sometimes wild swings (almost like ordinary shares) in the prices of junk bonds in response to seemingly small interest-rate changes.

Inflation Risk

This is the most insidious risk for all types of investments, but its effect is often most stark in the bond markets. Also referred to as *purchasing power risk*, it is the risk that the money – interest and principal – the investor receives on a bond will buy fewer and fewer goods and services, like food, clothing, petrol, and property, over time. In short, prices rise and the value of your money declines. Since October 2006, the purchasing power of every pound you own has dropped to 84p. Imagine the effect of inflation on your savings or low-return investments over your lifetime.

In order for the value of your money to keep pace with inflation, your return has to be equal to the rate of inflation. In truth the return has to be higher than inflation because of taxes you will pay on the gains. Investing too conservatively in low-interest, safe bonds may preserve the face value of your capital; however, if inflation rises significantly (as many experts predict will due to the government's actions during the financial crisis) then the real value of your money in the marketplace will certainly decline.

Reinvestment Risk

This is the risk that an investor will not be able to reinvest the money he or she makes on a bond at the same rate that he or she is currently receiving as a coupon payment. In recent years, many people became aware of this risk during the period when the Bank of England set the base rate to historically low levels. Suddenly they could no longer get the old rate they received on money in savings and other fixed-rate accounts. Investors react by looking for any investment or account that will pay a higher risk-free or low-risk return. As a result, many put their money at greater risk (by investing in shares, for example), without really understanding the potential loss involved.

It's important to keep in mind that there's no such thing as a risk-free investment or a guaranteed-return investment. Zero-coupon bonds are subject to the most reinvestment risk because an investor gets all of the cash flows at the end when the bond matures.

Call Risk

Some bonds contain a call provision that gives the issuer the right to redeem (buy back) the bond from the holder, usually at a specified price and during or after a specified period of time. A corporation is likely to call its bonds when interest rates are going down. The company will redeem the old bonds on which it is paying a higher-than-market rate of interest. Investors will get their money back and will most likely only be able to reinvest it at a much lower rate. Call risk is therefore directly associated with reinvestment risk. To help reduce investors' concerns about call risk, many companies issue bonds with a period of call protection. During this time, typically the first five years after the bond is issued, the company cannot buy back the bond. Thus investors know how long they will be able to receive the bond's interest payments before they are likely to stop because the company calls the bond.

Liquidity Risk

This is the risk that a security can only be sold by paying high transaction fees and other costs. Short-term fixed-income securities with investment-grade ratings are most in demand among investors of all types – retail and institutional – and are therefore the most liquid, that is, the easiest to buy and sell. In contrast, long-term bonds with declining or poor creditworthiness will have fewer investors interested in buying them. This lack of demand results in a wider bid–offer spread and there may higher commissions charged to execute the trades since it will be difficult to find a counterparty. Such a bond is described as illiquid.

Political Risk

This risk was demonstrated when the US Congress reached an impasse on raising the debt ceiling. If it had not been resolved, then the US could have defaulted on its debt payments for the first time in history. Another manifestation of political risk would be if a country suddenly decided to nationalise all private businesses. Any debt or equity securities would be worthless. (Within a country, this is often referred to as *legislative risk*.) It is widely believed that political risk was a significant factor in Standard & Poor's downgrading of US government debt.

Rewards Of Investing In Bonds

There are three potential rewards of directly investing in bonds and other fixed-income securities.

The first reward is the stream of interest payments. Assuming that the corporation, government, or other issuer of a bond does not default, an investor who purchases a bond with a fixed coupon rate knows how much interest he or she will receive at regular intervals until the bond matures or until it is called (if it has a call provision). Depending on the individual's cash-flow needs, he or she can buy bonds that pay interest at different six-month periods so that payments are received every month, every two months or every quarter. Again, the amount and frequency an investor sets up depends on his or her individual needs. These fixed returns on bonds can help to smooth the variable cash flows of dividend payments from equities.

The second reward is the payment of the bond's principal or nominal value at maturity. On a fixed date, the corporation or government pays (or repays if the bond was issued at par value) £100 (or multiples thereof) to the bondholder. Regardless of how interest rates fluctuate and, in turn, inversely affect the market price of fixed-income securities, the investor has the option of holding the bond to its maturity. [Note: This is not true of bond funds. They have a perpetual maturity because the fund managers are continually buying bonds into and selling them out of the portfolio.]

Understand that payment of principal is not guaranteed because of the issuer's risk of default. However, investment-grade bonds are among the least likely to default, so receiving these bonds' principal at maturity can be considered a reasonable certainty. Once the investor receives this amount, he or she can choose to invest in another bond, and when to do so. Such a strategy would be typical of someone whose investment objective is preservation of capital. Importantly, this is when reinvestment risk is most likely to become starkly clear. As investors seek to reinvest their money, they may find that comparable investment products with similar risk profiles pay lower interest rates – sometimes substantially lower. Investors for whom safety and preservation of capital are their utmost objectives are sometimes willing to accept the lower interest rates because of the reasonable certainty of getting back the money they had invested – something that is much less certain with ordinary shares of any type.

The third potential reward is available to investors who are interested in trading bonds, particularly high-yield or junk bonds, zero-coupon bonds, or bonds with long-term maturities. These bonds are among the most volatile of all types of traditional fixed-income securities. Depending on expectations about future interest-rate changes, the prices of these bonds may swing up and down by percentages that are more often associated with equities. Such gyrations present an opportunity to make capital gains – buying the bond at a low price and then selling it later at a higher price, or selling short the bond at a high price and buying it back later at a lower price. This is what sophisticated bond traders do to profit from interest-rate changes. It's probably not a strategy that would be appropriate to most investors who typically view bonds as a 'retreat to safety' not as an opportunity for speculative profits.

Investing directly in individual bonds is not the same as investing in a bond fund. While a unit trust, OEIC, or investment trust can give an individual investor instant diversification across many types of bonds with different risk profiles and different maturity dates, the structure of the portfolio is determined by the investment manager. He or she determines the interest payment and maturity dates of the bonds in the fund's portfolio, and both can change frequently as the manager sells old bonds and buys new ones, at his or her discretion. (Investors only find out about the changes after the fact.) So bond funds don't actually provide exactly the same fixed-income stream at regular intervals as a self-structured bond portfolio would and they don't have a fixed maturity date. Instead, they are perpetual. These characteristics may not be perfectly aligned with your individual investment objectives. Structuring one's own portfolio of individual bonds as a component of a comprehensive, diversified investment strategy can add greater transparency (regarding cash flows and pricing), control (especially as it relates to maturities and costs), and market insights, which can ultimately help investors achieve their individual investment goals more effectively.

Bond Market For Retail Investors: Order Book for Retail Bonds (ORB)

In the UK, the bond markets have historically been institutional. There was a small vibrant retail market many years ago, but it died unexpectedly with the widespread introduction of the Eurobond in the United Kingdom. This began in the early 1960s when Autostrade, the Italian State Highway Authority, issued the first Eurobond. Today, few individual investors buy bonds directly, especially corporate bonds, mostly due to the minimum purchase amount required – typically £50,000. Also, there is the additional factor that bonds, unlike equities, do not produce the get-rich-quick gains. However, during periods when people are concerned about reducing their exposure to the volatility and risks associated with equities, yet at the same time want to earn a better yield than they would on gilts, many small retail investors have become interested in corporate bonds.

Recognising this increasing, and relatively new interest

from individuals, the London Stock Exchange launched its Order Book for Retail Bonds (ORB) trading platform in February 2010. ORB offers access to gilts as well as a larger number of corporate bonds, with the minimum denomination of the purchase being £1,000.

ORDER BOOK FOR RETAIL BONDS

TIDM	Name	Coupon	Mat date	Price	Wks Chng	Yield	Gross Red Yld	Period of Coupon
AE57	Aviva	6.125	14/11/36	80.5	1.95	7.943	12.29	12 mth
AA18	Barclays Bank	5.75	14/09/26	77.62	1.26	8.456	9.78	12 mth
59VB	BP Capital Markets	4	29/12/14	105.68	0.01	2.055	2.82	12 mth
42PU	British Telecom Nts	8.5	07/12/16	122.59	0.50	2.606	4.35	12 mth
AG99	GlaxoSmithKline Cap	5.25	19/12/33	115.67	1.78	4.157	13.4	6 mth
AR96	Imperial Tobacco Fin	6.875	13/06/12	102.44	-0.07	1.868	0.5	12 mth
81CE	Legal & General	5.875	31/12/99	79.25	-1.50	7.416	13.54	6 mth
LBG1	Lloyds TSB Bank Snr	5.375	07/09/15	100.91	-0.10	5.102	3.38	6 mth
LBG2	Lloyds TSB Bank Snr	5.5	25/09/16	100.25	0.62	5.438	4.22	6 mth
NG1Q	National Grid	1.25(var)	06/10/21	102	0.47	0	0	6 mth
PFP5	Places For People	5	27/12/16	105.43	-0.60	3.806	4.42	6 mth
PFG7	Provident Fin	7	14/04/20	103.88	0.00	6.391	6.4	6 mth
PF16	Provident Fin	7.5	30/09/16	105.63	-1.12	6.125	4.06	6 mth
RB51	Royal Bank of Scotland	5.1	01/02/20	86.98	0.41	7.274	6.53	12 mth
RBI2	Royal Bank of Scotland	2	07/11/18	95.09	-1.04	2.792	6.5	12 mth
92OD	Safeway	6.5	05/08/14	110.85	-0.32	2.221	2.46	12 mth
TS52	Tesco	5.2	24/08/18	107	-0.25	3.997	5.66	6 mth
31CL	Tesco	5.5	13/12/19	113.5	1.38	3.533	6.71	12 mth
40OS	Tesco	6	14/12/29	119.35	-0.45	4.419	11.87	12 mth
VO32	Vodafone	5.9	26/11/32	115.59	1.46	4.712	12.93	12 mth
88ZJ	Wal-Mart Stores	4.75	29/01/13	104.32	-0.02	0.886	1.09	6 mth

Data provided by the London Stock Exchange. Please see http://www.londonstockexchange.com/retail-bond-prices for a comprehensive list of Retail Bonds.
Data compiled on: December 9th 2011

Figure 5-3. The Listing for Corporate Bonds traded on ORB. This column, Figure 5-3, published daily in the *Financial Times*, lists the bonds that were bought and sold on the London Stock Exchange's trading platform, Order Book for Retail Bonds (ORB). Beginning with the securities' Tradable Instrument Display Mnemonic (TIDM) which identifies the specific bond issue, the listing shows each issue's coupon rate, maturity date, closing market price, yield to redemption, duration (Gross Red Yld) and frequency of the bond's coupon payments.

One of the benefits of ORB is that a corporation or other entity issuing bonds can diversify its capital-raising base beyond institutional investors (e.g. pension funds, unit trust companies, etc.). Companies like Lloyds Bank TSB, Tesco, and others listed in Figure 5-3 that would normally have marketed their bond offering only to institutions, have found a strong response from individual investors on ORB. In fact, the strong demand has resulted in 1) companies being able to raise more capital than the minimum target they had initially sought in their offering programme; or 2) the new offering programme closing earlier than expected because the business raised the capital more quickly than it originally planned. This strong demand indicates two important recognitions among individual investors in the low-interest-rate environment that was the case as I was writing this book: 1) that individual bonds, as an asset class, have features and characteristics that offer more control and clarity over such things as the timing of cash flows, maturities, and reinvestment; and 2) that high-quality corporate bonds can be the source of a higher yield – both the coupon rate and YTR – without substantially increasing the risk associated with the overall investment portfolio.

6

POOLED INVESTMENTS:
UNIT TRUSTS, OEICs,
INVESTMENT TRUSTS
AND ETFs

A pooled investment, commonly called a *fund*, is a type of asset in which individuals or institutions with the same investment objectives buy into a portfolio of shares, bonds, or both. Described from a different perspective, investors' monies are 'pooled' together by the fund's creator and used to buy a diverse group of securities, called a *portfolio*, that seeks to achieve a stated investment objective.

The widespread popularity of funds comes from the three benefits they offer, especially to small investors. First, they give the investor access to professional investment managers whom individuals might not otherwise be able to afford. This is especially true for first-time investors and those with modest amounts of money. A fund's portfolio manager (or its team of managers) typically has relevant professional qualifications, usually including university degrees in business, that demonstrate in-depth training in finances, securities analysis, investment strategies and asset allocation among various kinds of investments. Paying for such expertise individually would be costly. In a fund, however, these costs are spread over everyone in the pool, which significantly lowers the cost for each investor.

The second benefit of funds is that they typically offer easy access to a diversified portfolio of securities. For most investors, it is quite expensive to buy a sufficient number of individual shares and bonds to achieve diversification that substantially reduces stock-specific risk – that is, the risk of loss due to the price decline of a single type of security or a single company's securities. Recent research has demonstrated that an individual investor who owns as few as ten to fifteen carefully chosen stocks and bonds in different business sectors would significantly lower stock-specific risk. While buying this relatively small number of different shares and/or bonds might not be exorbitant, the amount of time an investor would spend doing research and creating the right mix of securities would be. Because a fund pools many investors' monies, it has the financial resources needed to research, analyse, and acquire sufficient quantities of securities in different business sectors to achieve diversification. A fund's portfolio can contain securities by several hundred different issuers. Therefore, regardless of how little or how large the amount a person has to invest in a fund, he or she instantly attains diversification upon buying the fund's shares.

The third benefit of funds is lower investment costs. The commissions associated with buying and selling individual shares and bonds can add up to a significant amount. When subtracted from any gains made on these investments, these commissions lower the total return. With a fund, the commissions and other trading costs are spread across the hundreds or thousands of investors in the pool and therefore should be lower for each investor. However, this may not always be the case. Many funds have ongoing annual fees and expenses. While these may be deducted from the fund a little each day, over time these can add up to a significant cost – and a drag on the fund's total return, and hence the return each investor makes. The total percentage of these annual costs, known as the total expense ratio (TER) or ongoing charges figure (OCF), varies with each fund but it is one of the most important factors to evaluate before investing in a fund. It directly affects the profits you make.

Financial services companies, such as investment banks, investment companies, commercial banks or brokerage firms create funds with different business structures (for example, unit trusts, investment trusts, open-end investment companies), which they then market to potential investors. A very popular fund can grow to have tens of thousands of shareholders who have put in hundreds of millions of pounds. However, the creator or sponsor of a fund and its Board of Directors may decide it has become too big to be managed effectively to continue delivering attractive returns. They may therefore close the fund to new investors. However, people who already own the share can continue to invest more money.

Most financial service companies create multiple types of funds, sometimes called a *family of funds*. This approach aims to appeal to and capture the pounds from a wide array of investors with different goals and different asset allocation strategies. Each fund has a stated investment objective. This describes or reflects 1) the specific strategy that will be used by the portfolio manager (if there is one); and 2) the types of securities that will be bought into the fund's portfolio using investors' money. The illustration opposite lists some of the objectives that pooled investments have.

Figure 6-1: These charts list some of the most common fund objectives. The creators or sponsors of funds are continually creating new funds to attract new investors and to profit from ever-changing market trends.

Understanding a fund's objective as well as how it will be accomplished is an important consideration. An objective of capital growth or income, for example, can be achieved by different portfolio managers in distinctly different ways.

Is there a portfolio manager or an investment adviser employed by every fund? No. A fund is either managed or unmanaged. A *managed fund* is one in which a fund manager – who can be an individual or a group of trained professionals that includes a portfolio manager, analysts and researchers – chooses the securities to buy into and sell out of the fund's portfolio. As stated earlier, these choices must be in keeping with a stated investment objective, which is set by the financial institution that creates the fund. This type of fund usually has higher annual expenses due primarily to the management fee (typically the largest expense of a managed fund). There are also additional commission costs depending on how frequently securities are bought and sold, if such activities are in keeping with the fund's objectives.

An *unmanaged fund* does not have a portfolio manager to make the buy-and-sell decisions. The objective of this type of pooled investment is to track the exact performance – both the price movement and the dividend return – of a specific broad-based index such as 1) the FTSE 250; 2) a narrow-based index that follows a particular business sector or group of securities (such as a transportation index made up of a specific selection of companies involved in transport); or 3) a customised index that tracks the movement of the investments market in a specific country or a group of related markets in a region or around the world. Funds with this objective are more widely referred to as *tracker funds, index funds* or *passive funds.*

In this type of fund, the only time a new security is bought into or an existing security is sold out of the portfolio is when the creator of the index changes the composition of the actual index. Each index has its own set timetable (annually, semi-annually, quarterly, etc) of when changes are announced to the public and then implemented. Basically, the creator of the index removes securities that no longer qualify and replaces them with new ones that do. At that time, the fund that tracks that specific index sells those securities that have been removed and replaces them with the new ones that have been added. Because there is no active management of a tracker fund's portfolio and the turnover of securities in the portfolio is low, this type of pooled investment usually has relatively low ongoing annual expenses.

Funds are additionally described as being either *diversified* or *non-diversified.* In general, a high percentage of a diversified fund's investments must be held in a broad range of securities. Rules governing investment trusts and regulated funds specify the maximum percentage of the funds assets that can be concentrated in any one security. This provision is designed to prevent undue concentration of the fund's money in one issuer's security, which would increase the portfolio's exposure to the risk of having 'too many eggs in one basket'. Funds that exceed the regulations' maximum concentration limits are non-diversified. These tend to be unregulated non-mainstream investments.

It's not important for you, the investor in a fund, to be familiar with all the specific regulatory requirements of pooled investments. However, it is important to know the specific details that each fund must reveal to every customer before he or she invests. This information is disclosed in a Key Investor Information Document (KIID) that every fund must issue under EU regulations and that anyone considering buying a fund must receive and read. This document must be in a standardised format and free of jargon and complex terminology. In addition to all of the practical information about a fund KIID provides, it tells an investor in clear language 1) which company created the fund and the name of the manager or team responsible for managing the portfolio; 2) the fund's investment objective and how it will attempt to achieve it; 3) whether the fund is managed or unmanaged; 4) the risk and reward profile of the fund, 5) the fund's charges; and 6) its past performance. All fees (entry charges, exit charges, etc.) are itemised in KIID as are all on-going annual expenses you will pay on the money you invest. Pay careful attention to the total expense ratio (TER) or ongoing charges figure (OCF) – i.e. what a fund charges investors annually who have money in the fund – and the total annual return (calculated using a standardised formula). The return should be evaluated over several years in order to be useful. Three to five years is a good benchmark. Investing in a fund without such a track record involves more risk because there is no historical information about its performance. In such a situation, you need to pay even more careful attention to the portfolio manager's history. Has he or she managed other funds and what returns were produced during the manager's tenure? Again, always look carefully at the total expense ratio (or ongoing charges figure). The larger a fund's total annual expenses, the higher the return needed to cover those costs and produce a positive return for investors. In pursuing a high return, the portfolio manager may have to take risks that are unsuitable for your tolerance.

Keep in mind, however, that any historical information and current data, whether for a fund with a long history or a new fund, are no guarantee of future returns. At the bottom line, all of this information is disclosed – that is, made public – so that you can be a more informed investor, judging for yourself the potential risks and rewards of a fund.

Understanding a Fund's Value and Price

Each fund consists of a managed or unmanaged portfolio of securities. Each share or unit of a fund bought by an investor presents an undivided, small percentage of the total value of that underlying portfolio. It gives the owner the right to participate in the rise and fall of the total value of the portfolio, as well as to receive a part of any total investment income (dividends or interest) that the securities in the portfolio pay out.

Traditionally, the net asset value (NAV) of a fund was computed at the end of each business day after the LSE closed. Today, however, the bulk of UK-domiciled open-ended funds (unit trusts and OEICs) are valued at 12 noon GMT each business day. This is often referred to as the valuation point. Only a small minority of fund management groups still choose to value at 5 pm GMT after the LSE has closed or at 4 pm EST after the US markets have closed. The price used by this remaining small group of funds for each share, bond, or other security in the portfolio is its final price (referred to as the closing price) when trading ends on the primary exchange or other markets where it trades.

The NAV is always calculated and stated *per share* – i.e. for each share of the fund that has been sold to investors. The calculation is relatively simple. First, the market values at noon of all securities in the portfolio are totalled. Then a small percentage of various annual and ongoing expenses, such as the management fees and operating expenses (commissions, administrative costs, custodial fees, directors' fees, etc.) are deducted. (These amounts are essentially divided proportionately over the fund's fiscal year.) Finally, the remaining net amount is divided by the total number of a fund's outstanding shares.

The company that manages the fund does not perform the price calculation. Instead, each fund is required to have a trustee bank or custodian bank that holds and safeguards the portfolio, calculates the fund's *net asset value* (NAV), and disseminates this information to the market.

A fund's NAV changes daily due to two factors. The first is the value of the stocks, bonds and other securities in the portfolio. As they collectively rise and fall each day, so will the fund's NAV. The second factor is the number of the fund's shares that are outstanding – i.e. held by investors. This is referred to as a fund's *capitalisation.* Some pooled investments, such as an investment trust, have a relatively fixed capitalisation. Many usually issue shares only once or quite infrequently; however, this is not always the case. The capitalisation of other types of funds, unit trusts and OEICs being the prime example, vary from day to day, as a fund issues new shares when investors put more money into the fund and redeems (buys back) shares when investors want to sell – i.e. pull their money out of the fund.

The market price at which a person buys into a fund may or may not be directly related to the NAV. This all depends on the structure of the fund and will be explained in the next section, which looks at the four types of funds available in the UK.

And finally, remember that a fund's NAV is typically calculated at one point during the day. Currently the valuation point is 12 noon GMT. With the widespread use of powerful computers in the markets, this all changed. Today, computers can be programmed to calculate, in microseconds, a fund's NAV in real time throughout the day while the securities in the portfolio are being actively traded. Given that some funds hold hundreds of different securities, this is an amazing capability. This development led to the creation of a new type of fund whose shares can be traded on a stock exchange, like an ordinary share, at a price equal to or very close to the fund's dynamic NAV throughout the day. It is called an *exchange-traded fund* (ETF) and is explained in the next section. It is no exaggeration to say that ETFs revolutionised how people invest. Importantly, ETFs also spurred the creation of new products that changed with the types of products, called equities. New variations of ETFs include products that are regulated as commodities, such as gold, silver, crude oil and heating oil. The new versions, called *exchange-traded commodities* (ETCs), have brought about what some professionals call the 'equitisation of commodities'. For the first time, traditional stock investors have access to commodities through an investment vehicle that is the equivalent of an ordinary share. Pooled investments have moved way beyond a simple portfolio of stocks managed by an investment professional.

The Types of Pooled Investments

There are four types of pooled investments. Their basic structures share many similarities. Among them, each fund has a stated investment objective, a portfolio of securities that is either managed or unmanaged and a trustee or depository (in the case of an OEIC) that actually holds and safeguards the securities in the portfolio as well as calculates the NAV and market price of the fund at the valuation point each business day. The three key features distinguishing one type of fund from another are 1) the way market values (the prices at which they can be bought and sold) are determined; 2) how the fees and other costs are charged, and 3) how they are bought and sold. [Note: I'm deliberately avoiding using the word *traded* here because not all funds offer tradable securities (units or shares) to investors.]

Unit Trust

When a person buys a *unit trust*, he or she receives units of the trust's portfolio. The number of units an individual acquires is determined by dividing the amount of money he or she is investing by the market price per unit at that time.

	Bid	Offer	+/-	Yield
Schroder Income A Inc	725.70	770.50	-3.80	4.48
Schroder Income A Acc	4481.00	4758.00	-23.00	4.40

Figure 6-2: Example of a newspaper listing for two unit trusts by Schroder Investment Management Limited. In a typical listing of unit trusts the management companies are shown in alphabetical order and then under each company's name is listed each of its unit trusts in alphabetical order. The prices are in pence unless otherwise indicated. After the name of the

[unit, the first column of numbers is the bid price (a customer's selling price); the second is the offer price (a customer's buying price); the third shows the positive or negative change compared with the previous day's bid price; and the final column shows the fund's year-to-date (YTD) yield, taking into account any buying or selling expenses.]

Unit-trust quotes consist of two prices: the selling price (also called the *bid price*) and the buying price (called the *offer price*). When an investor puts money into a unit trust, that purchase is made at the fund's offer price. When a person wants to sell unit-trust shares he or she already owns, the sale is executed at the fund's bid price. In reality, this sale is actually a redemption because the fund buys back the shares itself. Hence, unit trusts are considered to be redeemable securities, not tradable securities. As mentioned in the previous section, the majority of UK authorised funds calculate their price at the 12 noon GMT valuation point every business day. If a customer places an order before noon, then he or she will deal at that day's calculated price. If an order comes in after 12 noon (for example at 2 pm GMT), then the order will be executed at the next business day's 12 noon valuation price. When placing an order a customer will not know the exact purchase or redemption price until the next valuation point. This convention is known as forward pricing.

As the value of the securities in the trust's portfolio rise and fall, so will the market price of the units. When people invest additional money in the fund, the manager simply issues more units and uses the investors' money to buy more shares into the portfolio. When an investor wants to sell (or redeem) his or her units, the manager buys them back and gives the shareholder their value in cash. Most funds keep some of their assets in cash to be able to pay for these redemptions without being forced to sell shares from the underlying portfolio. Otherwise the fund would have to liquidate some of the securities in the portfolio in order to get the needed cash to pay investors for their redemptions. As a result of these purchases and redemptions, the number of units outstanding changes continually from day to day. A unit trust therefore does not have a fixed capitalisation.

As Figure 6-2 shows, the buying price (the offer) is always higher than the selling price (the bid) for a unit. This is because the upfront sales for a unit charges are incorporated into the offer price, as are other costs (such as the bid-offer spreads on the securities in the portfolio, stamp duty, and any marketing and distribution expenses). An investor will usually pay the maximum initial or upfront sales charge when buying unit-trust shares directly from the management company that created the trust. However, if a customer is investing a substantial lump sum at one time, the company will reduce the initial sales charge or rebate a portion of it.

There are other ways to reduce this upfront fee. Discount brokers sell unit trusts for a one-time fee, which is almost always a lower amount than the full initial sales charge. And financial advisers who charge by the hour usually rebate to the investor the portion of the initial sales charge they receive as compensation from the management company.

Earlier in this chapter, I mentioned that there were many other costs (for example, stockbrokerage and custodial fees) that are deducted a little each day. These are factored into the calculation of the trust's bid price. Of these, the most important is the annual charge. It is the largest part of what is known as a unit trust's *total expense ratio* or ongoing charges figure – i.e. the total percentage of the fund's value charged over the course of each year by the investment manager and other entities (such as the fund's depository bank, the trading firms that execute the buy and sell order for securities in the portfolio, etc.) for their services. Each year the portfolio manager (if it's a managed fund) or the stock market (if it's an unmanaged fund) has to produce a big enough return for investors in the fund to recover the annual charge, as well as all of the other ongoing annual fees, before it can produce a profit. Year on year, this and other charges can be a substantial drag on a unit trust's performance, especially in a flat or bearish market. In fact, in a bearish market the charges only make the negative return worse.

In the fund world, paying higher expenses rarely gets you a better return. It is prudent to choose a fund with a low total expense ratio, given the type of fund in which you are investing, so that a larger percentage of the profits end up in your bank account.

Investors should avoid buying a unit trust based on one year's performance. As the disclaimer about unit trusts and other funds clearly states, 'Past performance is not a guide to the future.' A more prudent strategy is to examine the fund's performance over at least a three-year period, but preferably a five- to ten-year period. Compare the performance to the fund's benchmark index. You want to see performance that is consistently better than the index in both bull and bear markets. Also check the tenure of the portfolio manager. You need to verify that the same person or team managed the portfolio during this period and is therefore responsible for this return. If the manager or team is no longer in charge of the fund, then the long-term performance numbers will not serve as a good reference point.

And finally, investors will want to consider how much risk is associated with a unit trust relative to the returns it provides. Ideally, investors want to see above-average returns combined with below-average risk or volatility. This is also referred to as the *risk-adjusted return*. One measure of how a fund's performance compares to its risk profile is known as the *Sharpe ratio*. The higher the Sharpe ratio, the less risk the portfolio manager took on to produce the reported total return. Stated another way, the significant return was more likely due to smart investing on the part of the portfolio manager, rather than the result of his or her buying higher-risk securities.

Most of the information you or any investor needs to assess a particular unit trust, including the Sharpe ratio, can be found at the website www.morningstar.com. For each unit trust, this company provides a summary sheet of data about performance (current, historic, and compared to the fund's benchmark), total return, fees, portfolio composition, the portfolio manager and more. This should be a basic reference item for anyone interested in or already invested in unit trusts. It also has its own proprietary five-star rating system, which can make the entire evaluation process much easier for potential investors. Also remember the Key Investor Information Document (KIID) must disclose much of the same information.

Open-Ended Investment Companies (OEICs)

Widely referred to as 'oiks', OEICs are a simpler version of a unit trust and were introduced into the UK in the late 1990s. This type of fund is set up as a limited liability company, instead of as a trust. Therefore OEICs issue shares instead of units (as a trust does). Like a unit trust, an OEIC's capitalisation – i.e. the number of shares outstanding – changes each business day in response to investors' purchases and redemptions. An OEIC must stand ready each business day to issue new shares and redeem old shares. This is why, like a unit trust, it is described as being open-ended.

In addition to the basic structure of the fund, the other key difference between a unit trust and an OEIC is how the latter's price is quoted. An OEIC has only one price. It does not have a bid price and an offer price (see Figure below). An OEICs single price is calculated at 12 noon GMT each business day, this single price reflecting the *net asset value* of each outstanding share.

	Bid	Offer	+/-	Yield
M&G Recovery GBP A Inc	114.97	-	-0.98	0.93
M&G Recovery GBP A Acc	249.93	-	-2.13	0.93

Figure 6-3: Example of a newspaper listing two OEICs by M&G Investments. As with all OEICs, there is only one price, which is shown in the bid column. The single price is calculated at the 12 noon GMT valuation point. It is both a OEIC's buying (offer) price and its selling (bid) price. Other charges are added to (for a purchase) or subtracted from (for a redemption) this single price separately. The third column shows the positive or negative change over the previous day's valuation point price. The forth column shows year-to-date return, taking into account any buying or selling costs.

When a person buys or redeems OEIC shares, the price at which the order is executed uses the forward pricing convention. If the customer enters the order before noon, the customer gets that day's price calculated at the noon valuation point. If the order is entered after noon, the person gets the price computed at 12 noon GMT the next day. The initial sales charge or commission is then added to the purchase price or subtracted from the sale proceeds.

Many unit trusts are now converting to the OEIC one-price model. It's easier for investors to understand adding or subtracting a charge or commission rather than having it built into the purchase price. Both investment products are suitable for long-term investing, not short-term speculation.

Investment Trusts

To create an investment trust, a management company issues shares of the specific trust it is creating to the public (retail and institutional) to raise the money it will pool together to buy the corporate and/or government securities in the trust's portfolio. Instead of being backed by a corporation's assets as ordinary shares are, an investment trust's shares are backed only by the securities in the portfolio. Like other funds, the portfolio can consist of the securities of companies that trade in a specific foreign market (such as the stock exchange in Malaysia or South Africa), region (e.g. Latin America) or a particular business sector.

Traditionally, an investment trust issues a fixed number of shares to the public. The fund then closes its doors, so to speak, and for the most part does not issue any new shares or buy back any outstanding shares. Investment trusts are therefore said to have a *fixed capitalisation* – relatively. If, for example, the trust proves very popular, its management company *may* issue more shares; if the fund proves to be a laggard, the trust *may* choose to buy back some of its shares. [Note: Today it is commonplace for an investment trust whose underlying portfolios consist of liquid securities to buy back its own shares and issue additional shares depending on the value of the trust's shares on the stock exchange.] A trust is under no obligation to do either of these. This is completely different from a unit trust and an OEIC, whose funds are open-ended – i.e. they are continually issuing new shares and buy back old shares in response to customer orders to buy (put money into) or redeem (pull money out of) the fund, respectively.

Shares of an investment trust trade on a stock exchange – again, exactly like ordinary shares. Therefore, they can be correctly described as tradeable securities. This is an important distinction. Unit trusts and OEICs do not issue tradable securities. Instead, they issue securities (units and shares) that are redeemable. They do not trade on a stock exchange or on any trading market. They can only be bought from and sold back to the unit trust or OEIC itself, or through one of the fund's authorised sales agents – other financial institutions that have written agreements to sell the same funds. While many people think they are trading unit trusts and OEICs, in reality they are not.

Because investment trust shares do trade in the secondary market – i.e. on a stock exchange or other organised trading market – their prices are quoted like ordinary shares. There is a bid price and an offer price that change continually throughout the day. These market prices may have no relationship to actual net asset value (NAV) per share of the securities in the investment trust's portfolio. However, the trust's NAV is referenced to indicate if the current price is *above* the NAV (trading at a premium), *below* the NAV (trading at a discount), or, even more rare, *at* the NAV (trading at par).

The market price of an investment trust's shares depends totally on investors' expectations about the future economic growth in that specific country, region or business sector. Immediately after being issued, you would think the trust would trade at a slight discount because of the various underwriting and other fees that are built into the issue price of the shares. It seems logical that the market would immediately reduce the market value of the shares to reflect the payout of these costs by the trust. In fact, most new investment trust offerings trade at a small premium. This is because the issuing brokers tend to support the price in the early days after it begins trading.

Investment trusts make money in three ways. First, the securities in the trust may pay dividends (equities) and/or interest (bonds). This investment income, minus certain administrative expenses, is distributed to shareholders. Secondly, a share's market price may rise due to positive expectations about the future performance of the investments in the trust. When the shares are sold, the investor will realise a capital gain. Conversely, if investors become pessimistic about the future returns of the securities in the portfolio, the market price of the investment trust shares will trade at a deeper and deeper discount to the underlying portfolio's NAV. Thirdly, the price of an investment trust's shares can rise towards their usually higher NAV. (Most investment trusts trade at a discount to their NAV after the issuing brokers stop supporting the price.) When this happens, the discount between the market price and the NAV narrows or become smaller, yielding a profit.

Investment trusts have a way of increasing the returns from their investment portfolios that other funds don't have. It's called *leverage*. FSA Regulations permit each investment trust to borrow an amount up to a fixed percentage of the trust's total net asset value (NAV). A fund can use this borrowing to buy more securities into its portfolio, thereby increasing the potential return that shareholders may receive. Leverage also increases the amount of loss a trust can experience in a bear market. Most investment trusts use this leverage.

Finally, remember that because shares from this type of fund trade on an exchange, you will pay a commission when buying or selling them. The amount will depend upon the type of broker you use. There's also a 0.50% stamp duty on all purchases. Investment trusts are perhaps the most complicated of all types of pooled investments and the true value of each one can sometimes be opaque. This is partly due to the fact that the market value of the trust's shares can at times seem completely disconnected from the value of the securities in the portfolio. More in-depth market knowledge and experience, as well as some sage, objective investment advice, seem both appropriate and necessary in order to be successful.

Exchange-Traded Funds (ETFs)

It is a widely known, well-documented fact in the financial markets that the vast majority of managed funds underperform in the overall stock market as measured by the FTSE 100 Index or FTSE All-Share Index. Given this statistic, it would seem reasonably unlikely that a novice investor would be able to choose a unit trust, OEIC or investment trust that could outperform the FTSE. This perception, combined with the difficulty many investors – new and experienced – have with understanding the various fees and expenses charged by most pooled investments, has made many people question the benefits of investing in a managed fund. Instead, they choose to invest in low-cost, unit trust or OEIC index funds, also called tracker funds. This way, the reasoning goes, the return on the money invested will be no less than that of the benchmark index. The pervasiveness of this point of view is reflected in the fact that the percentage of cash flows into tracker funds increases year on year in comparison to managed funds.

The popularity of tracker unit trusts and OEICs with investors, as well as some of their disadvantages, led the American Stock Exchange to create a new type of index investment product called an *index share, index participation unit* (IPU). Today, this product is known as an exchange-traded fund, or ETF. This product combines many of the attributes of a tracker unit trust or OEIC with those of an ordinary share. Like all pooled investments, there is an actual portfolio of securities that backs the ETF. This portfolio consists of the ordinary shares that make up the designated index – e.g. the FTSE 100 Index, the FTSE All-Share Index, the S&P 500 Index, Nasdaq 100 Index, or Dow Jones Industrial Average (DJIA). The portfolio is set up as a long-term trust and is held at a custodian bank. The composition of the portfolio only changes when the creator of the index (FTSE, Standard & Poor's, Dow Jones, MSCI) removes securities from, or adds them to the actual index.

Each individual ETF share represents a fractional portion (e.g. 1/20th, 1/100th, 1/1,000th) of the value of a designated index. The iShares FTSE 100 ETF, for example, is worth 1/1,000th of the value of the actual FTSE 100 index. While this fractional amount is fixed, the creator of the index can change the fraction. This could happen, for example, if the creator wanted to halve the market price of the ETF shares because their current market price was too high. This would in effect be a 1-for-1 stock split.

Overall, the number of units outstanding can remain relatively fixed. The quantity increases only when a large financial services institution, such as a brokerage firm or bank, working in conjunction with the ETF manager, deposits the amount of money into the trust needed to create a minimum number (e.g., 10,000 or 20,000) of new ETF shares. The specific amount of money is based on the market value of the securities that comprise the index on a given day. This money is immediately used to purchase those securities, and a new block of ETFs (representing a set fractional interest in the index) are issued and begin trading on an exchange.

Like most equity unity trusts and OEICs, most ETFs are diversified. The portfolio of securities replicates all of the shares in a designated index. Therefore, when an investor buys an ETF, he or she is investing in the whole market or sector. As noted earlier, diversification shields the individual's investment money against stock-specific risk – the risk of a severe decline in the price of any one issuer's securities or in any one sector. The money invested is not, however, protected against a price decline in the overall stock market.

As with a common stock, an investor can buy any quantity of an ETF he or she desires – 1, 25, 200, 1,000 shares, or a fixed sterling amount such as £1000 or £2,500. There is no minimum purchase amount. And, most importantly, index shares can be bought and sold at any time during the trading day. This feature is one of the two primary differences between an ETF and a tracker fund. Unit trust or OEIC funds are not tradable. One cannot buy and sell them during the day as one can a stock or a bond; instead, they are redeemable securities. All purchases and redemptions are executed based on the price determined at the 12 noon GMT valuation point. This means that if you hear that the market is declining sharply in the afternoon on a trading day and you place an order to sell your unit trust or OEIC holdings, your order will be executed at the price calculated at the next day's valuation point.

In contrast, ETFs can be bought or sold at any time during the standard trading day, giving investors greater flexibility. ETFs have a bid price and an offer price based on the demand for the ETF shares themselves. However, keep in mind that there is an underlying portfolio of securities, and one of the aims of an ETF is to closely or exactly track the net asset value (NAV) of the shares in the portfolio.

The trading of this ETF is made possible by powerful computers. The key to understanding the price of an ETF is to know that computers calculate and disseminate to the market the net asset value (NAV) of the underlying portfolio continuously throughout the day as the prices of the securities in the index-tracking portfolio change with each trade. At the same time, the market value of the ETF shares themselves are being diminished. Therefore it is immediately clear to traders and other professionals when the market price of an ETF is trading at a *premium* (above) to its NAV or at a *discount* (below) to its NAV. If and when either of these price differences develops, specialised traders called *arbitrageurs* simultaneously buy the undervalued security (either the ETF or a representative basket of the securities in the index) and sell short the overvalued security (again, either the ETF or a representative basket of the securities in the index) in order to profit from the temporary pricing aberration. The effect of this arbitrage brings the market price of the ETF back close to the NAV of the underlying portfolio. Thus, throughout the trading day, the shares of a specific ETF have a market price that is the same as, or very close to, the underlying portfolio's NAV at that moment. The bid/offer spread for ETFs tend to be narrower than they are for unit trusts, for example.

As with tracker funds, there is no management of an ETF's portfolio. The shares or other securities are bought into, or sold out of the portfolio only when the composition of the specific index changes. The frequency varies depending on the index. Some change their composition once a year; others do so more often – quarterly, for example. This means that an ETF has lower portfolio turnover, and overall has some of the lowest total expenses among all types of funds. Many are less than 0.50%; however, careful research can find some newer ETFs with a total expenses ratio of less than 0.20%.

Like their OEIC cousins, EFTs give investors a way of investing in the overall stock market, a specific sector or a particular country, without having to go through what is, for many investors, the arduous process of selecting a particular company. If, for example, you expect that the leading public companies in the Eurozone will perform well over a period of time, then you can buy an ETF based on an index, instead of constructing your own portfolio of individual securities.

Not only do ETFs closely match the performance of the specific index, they also deliver the dividend yield of the index. In all cases, shareholders receive periodic distributions that correspond to the net dividends that accrue in the underlying portfolio. (It is described as *net dividends* because the trust that holds the portfolio deducts some ongoing expenses.) The frequency of the dividend payments varies. Depending on how the ETF is structured, you can choose to receive the dividend in cash or reinvest the dividend in the ETF. It's important to look at specific provisions of ETFs on a case by case basis because your choices vary with each ETF.

The popularity of this product has spurred many innovations among investment managers as they seek to meet and anticipate the needs of institutional and regional investors. ETFs have expanded far beyond equities. There are now ETFs that enable investment in the stock markets of different countries or regions; in specific business sectors; in fixed-income securities (bonds); in real estate; in commodities such as gold and crude oil (known as *exchange-traded commodities* or ETCs in the UK). There are those that focus on ethical investing, green investing or Shariah-compliant investments. There are even ETFs that profit when the market declines (these are called *short ETFs*) and others that use leverage to enable investors to make double the return on the upward (long) and downward (short) movement of the market.

More types of ETFs are being created every day. Most are announced in the financial media or at the creator's own website. Some of the new LSE-listed ETFs are no longer the plain-vanilla ETFs like those described in this section. Many, like short ETFs and those that use leverage, deliver their returns using a derivative investment product in which an investment bank is the counterparty. It is important to check how some of the newer, more exotic ETFs achieve their returns. Their structures may involve considerable additional risks, especially counterparty risk that may not be suitable for you. Not all of the newly introduced ETFs will be successful. But when they are, the competing managers create their own version in order to try to capture some of the money that investors are pouring into the new ETF. That's why you see so many different managers offering ETFs that mimic the FTSE 100, for example. The difference often lies in the total expense ratio and whether the ETF's underlying portfolio fully replicates the composition of its designated index or selectively samples the index's components according to a mathematical formula. With ETFs, it is a case where less (as in a lower expense ratio) is more (as in money in your pocket).

Summary

For the majority of people, funds are a gentle way to invest because of the diversification and low costs that are inherent to most of the different types. Funds can also be used effectively to invest in a single business sector or a single country. If, for example, you believe that a particular sector – such as social networking, biotechnology, or consumer goods – will be the next hot investment area, you can buy a sector or specialty fund instead of having to research and determine what specific stocks in this area have the greatest potential for capital appreciation.

Unit trusts, OEICs and ETFs are the most popular, especially the unmanaged, tracker-fund versions. Keep in mind that diversification is not a magic pill that eliminates all risk. Additionally, some funds, like those that invest in a particular business sector or country, may not be well diversified. This increases your risk of loss.

When evaluating any fund, there are three key things to pay attention to. The first is the fund's *investment objective*. Remember that it indicates the primary type of securities in which the portfolio manager invests, as well as the primary way he or she seeks to make money for the shareholders. A particular fund manager may interpret the same objective quite differently from a manager at another fund. He or she may also use different criteria for analysing and selecting the securities in which to invest. As a result of these differences, you may look at a large-cap fund and a mid-cap fund and discover that both portfolios contain many of the same securities – or have few in common. The portfolio manager's investment style or philosophy determines which securities are bought and sold in a portfolio.

Second, pay attention to the fund's *total expense ratio*, as well as the upfront fee if there is one. Managed funds typically have the highest expenses because of the management fee. But even among unmanaged funds, the ratio can vary. The less you pay, the more of the fund's net income will end up in your pocket. If you are looking for the lowest-cost fund, which will perform at least as well as the overall market, then a tracker fund is probably most appropriate.

And finally, remember that the risks associated with a specific fund correspond to the collective character of the securities in the portfolio. Before you invest in a fund, ask yourself those questions that will help you define your investment objective, risk tolerance, time horizon, and desired return, given the risk you are willing to accept in order to realise your investment goal.

7

YOUR INVESTMENT STRATEGY

Before you begin to invest – before you use your first hundred pounds to buy shares, bonds, unit trusts, gold shares or any other vehicle, educate yourself about the markets. Know how they work, who the participants are, and what basic products are available. Even if you have only lightly perused those parts of the preceding chapters directly related to your investment interests, at least you are beginning with some knowledge or idea of what you are doing. Equally, or perhaps more importantly, is to know why you are doing it and what you want to achieve.

Simply saying that you want to make money is not sufficient. You need to ask yourself how you want to make the money you invest grow, and how much risk you're willing to take on in exchange for a reasonable chance (and it's only a chance) for the appreciation. Remember, past performance is no guarantee of future performance, and investing – much like good doctoring – is part science and part art (often more art than we really want to admit). Gathering and organising the data into a system is the science. The art is interpreting that information and understanding its implications.

Some people seem to be 'naturals', whose intuitions are far more likely to be right than wrong. (Think Warren

Buffett.) Other people can learn the art in a purely intellectual way but lack the gut instincts of those who 'feel' the markets. They may experience success less often. Still others understand many of the basics and enjoy investing, but still need or want guidance; they may enjoy partnering with an investment professional. Finally, some people, who are fully capable of learning, simply may prefer to abdicate all decisions to the professionals. You must be honest with yourself in determining which best describes you. That will make the next step, deciding the kind of broker to use, much easier.

All About Brokers

What Kind Of Broker Do You Need?

One of the first decisions you have to make is whether you are going to be a DIY investor or if you are going to use a broker or financial adviser. Regardless of whether you invest on your own or use a professional to advise you, all trades must be handled through a brokerage firm or through a stockbroker. Even if you place your orders online, they still go through a brokerage firm. The individual broker or the company's computer records the details of your buy or sell order and then routes it electronically to the appropriate market for execution. Once the order is executed, the broker reports the details of the execution back to you, including the amount of money you owe the firm (in the case of a purchase) or the money you will receive (in the case of a sale). The broker, whether it is a company or an individual, earns a commission for providing this service.

A broker provides other services as well. The firm

reviews the details of your account to make sure they are current and accurate, especially the specific securities in your account, the quantities, their market value, and the amount of your cash balances. The firm makes certain that any dividends or interest paid by securities that you own are correctly credited to your account. If a broker offers you specific investment advice, suggestions or guidance, these must be suitable for your financial situation, investment objective and risk tolerance. A good broker can be a valuable partner in helping you to create, manage and increase the value of your investment portfolio; however, not everyone wants such guidance.

There are three main types of brokers, each offering a different array of services:

- An *execution-only broker* simply handles the sale or purchase of shares or other securities at your request, whether online or on the phone. This type of broker does *not* offer investment advice. The firm's computer routes your order to the market (computer servers in many cases) where the shares are trading, and it is executed at the best-published prices (the highest bid on a sale or lowest offer on a purchase) available at the moment, regardless of the spread. There is no human being involved, and there is no attempt by the routing firm to reduce the spread (the difference between the bid and offer prices). It is literally one computer executing an order against another computer's prices. The term *black-box trading* refers to this type of trade execution. As always, the brokerage firm involved in the trade receives a small commission on each transaction. Today this is the cheapest way to trade (especially for DIY investors). Execution-only brokers

178

offer their services via the Internet and are referred to as *online brokers.*

- An *advisory broker* suggests investment ideas and other strategies for helping you increase the value of your investment portfolio and achieving your stated investment objectives. He or she should spend time getting to know you – your financial means, your investment objectives, your risk tolerance, investment preference, and long-term goals for the money you have invested. Most advisory brokers are employees of brokerage firms, which provide access to expert analytical information that would not be easy to acquire on your own, such as detailed analysis of a company's financial statements, the overall business sector in which the company operates, as well as the impact of the current economic cycle, interest rate changes, domestic inflation, and international events.

  An advisory broker sometimes offers an additional service that investors may not be aware of: they will negotiate with the dealers who display the best prices to try to negotiate a higher bid or a lower offer price than is being displayed on his or her trading screen. In effect, they try to narrow or reduce the spread in order to get the customer an even better price. This does not happen with an execution-only broker. An advisory broker will be more expensive than an execution-only broker, but if you take advantage of the expert service and information offered, you may find the additional fees can be worthwhile.

- A *discretionary broker* has written authority from you or someone authorised to act on your behalf, to decide what securities will be bought into and sold out of your account. The broker still has to fulfil the 'know your customer' rule. General investment goals, time horizons, risk tolerances and strategies are set in consultation with the client, but the broker is free to manage the portfolio in pursuit of those goals, making all the daily investment decisions without consulting the client. A discretionary broker's fees are usually a fixed percentage of the total value of the assets under management; however, he or she can also charge a commission per trade.

For most new investors who have little in-depth knowledge about shares, bonds, unit trusts or other types of securities, an advisory broker may be the best choice. Working with a good advisory broker can advance your financial education and open your mind to investment ideas you might otherwise never consider. In years to come, once you've become an experienced investor with a strong sense of your own preferences, trading strategies and investment style, you might consider switching to an execution-only broker and making the investment decisions yourself.

Working with a Broker

The first step in working with any broker is filling out the firm's new account forms. The forms and the information requested will vary depending on the broker-dealer's own internal rules and requirements. A typical form asks about your financial status, your investment goals, your risk tolerance, and where dividends (on stocks) or interest (on bonds) should be paid. Some firms may also request a copy of your passport to verify your identity, but not all do.

You'll also be asked about how you want the shares you own to be held. The most convenient choice is to leave your shares registered in the brokerage firm's official account, called a *nominee account*. By doing this, your broker will be able to sell them immediately when you choose. On the other hand, if you hold the actual share certificates yourself, you will have to post them to the broker first before they can be sold. Also, it makes sense to keep money in your brokerage account so that when you want to buy shares, the transaction can be processed straight away; otherwise, there may be delays in getting your trade (especially a purchase) executed. However, if you hold stock that has been paid for in your broker's nominee account, then the firm will generally let you buy additional shares without cash in the account. However, be sure that the funds are there by the settlement day. If they are not, be prepared to pay a penalty rate of interest similar to that charged on an unauthorised overdraft.

Brokers offer various fee structures. You may be faced with a choice between an annual fee for maintenance of your account, combined with a low commission on trades (a worthwhile combination if you intend to make a lot of transactions), or a higher commission on trades with no annual fee (better for those who trade rarely). You will also have to pay stamp duty of 0.50% on every share purchased. When you sell shares, you may have to pay capital gains tax on any profits. These fees and expenses must be taken into account if you plan to be an active trader.

Know Your Broker

Choosing a broker is a little like choosing a GP. Professional credentials are important, but so are personal qualities. It may take a few attempts to find a broker with whom you're comfortable. It's worth the effort. It won't benefit you to choose a broker with a wealth of investment experience and expertise if you find you have difficulty talking openly and honestly with him or her; it is important to know that you will be getting clear, understandable answers to your questions (even questions that you think may sound 'naïve' or 'dumb') and that you will be treated with respect.

You can start your search for a broker by asking friends, family and business acquaintances for personal recommendations. If you come up empty, the Association of Private Client Investment Managers and Stockbrokers (APCIMS) has a full list of UK brokers. (Visit www.apcims.co.uk for detailed information.) Call to talk with a few of them, first by telephone and then in a face-to-face meeting. I believe it is essential to actually meet the person who is going to work with you and your money.

Record your reactions to each broker you are considering. Pay attention to how you are treated, the tone of voice used when speaking to you, the way he or she listens to and responds to your questions, and how each broker makes you feel. Remember, you must have total confidence that this person is interested in working with you and is interested in helping you achieve your financial goals. And you want to know what importance the broker places on giving you good customer service.

When interviewing a prospective broker, it will help you if you prepare the following information in advance: 1) the questions you plan to ask during the meeting; 2) a clear statement of your short-term and long-term investment goals; 3) any important schedules or timetables that will impact your financial situation; 4) what kinds of risk you believe you can reasonably tolerate; and 5) the kinds of investments (blue-chip shares, foreign shares, corporate bonds, gilts, etc.) you think you may be interested in. Below are some questions that may not immediately come to mind, but which you must include in your list.

- Do you handle orders for all of the types of investments in which I am interested? (Note: Not all brokerage firms provide customers with the ability to invest in securities that trade outside the UK.)
- What fees do you charge? How do you earn your compensation?
- Do you charge an administrative fee for keeping shares in a nominee account and other services, such as handling dividends? If so, what is that fee?
- Is interest paid on cash held in my brokerage account? If so, what is the rate and how often does it change?
- How quick is your trade execution and reporting process?
- How soon will money be released into my account after I've sold shares?
- What kind of online services do you offer? For example, can I access and track my portfolio throughout the trading day?

You'll learn as much from the broker's *attitude* in reacting to your questions as you will from the specific answers given.

Online Brokers

If you are an investor who wants to make your own investment choices and pay the lowest commissions or dealing costs, then online brokerage is an appropriate choice for you. These companies give their customers the ability to submit their buy and sell orders to the brokerage firm's computers without ever having to talk to a real person. The brokerage firm's computers check each order to make sure it complies with the firm's own regulatory policies, as well as those of the industry and the particular stock market where the order will be executed. An order routing system then typically sends the order to a Retail Service Provider (RSP), where it is executed immediately against the displayed bid/offer prices. Once the trade is completed, an execution report will be sent to you showing that you have a position (either long or short), or that you have sold or bought in your position and are no longer invested in that company. You will also receive a trade confirmation or Contract Note specifying the amount due (after a buy order is executed) or the amount of the proceeds (after the execution of a sell order).

You, the individual investor, are in total control of your investment decisions. Some online brokerage firms, known as *online supermarkets*, offer a wide array of investment products, including shares, bonds, unit trusts, OEICs, etc. Some let each individual manage all of his or her investments, including ISAs, in a single account, thus making it easier to keep an eye on the growth of the portfolio. In essence, an online supermarket is one-stop shopping for financial products. And it makes it easier for you to create and monitor the asset allocation model that you've established for yourself.

Although online brokerage firms generally don't provide investment advice or recommendations, many supermarkets offer links to research websites where you can read expert opinions about shares, bonds, or other investments in which you may be interested or have already invested in. Some will e-mail you with pre-arranged alerts, such as when your shares reach the *stop-loss* price you have selected. Quite a few of the tools and services are similar to those available through a traditional, full-service broker, but are made available directly to the customer online.

Not everyone is psychologically suited for online, DIY investing. You won't have a broker or adviser to confer with when there are rumours of impending turmoil, prices are falling, and panic is beginning to set in. Lacking a human lifeline (beyond those postings on the online discussion boards), some people who invest online end up trading beyond their risk tolerance, either because they are caught up in a fantasy or frenzy of potential gains or desperately trying to recoup losses. You have to be in control of yourself in order to invest effectively online. Find a way to keep a sense of proportion about your investing and, more importantly, your impulses, which are often what trigger unfortunate decisions.

Taking Advice

At some point in your life, you may decide that you would like to work with a financial adviser or investment professional. Most people's finances are relatively straight forward that it may be useful to visit a financial adviser to help you establish, and then periodically review and adjust, your long-term financial plan. You can then usually implement these plans yourself. With today's wealth of financial information in newspapers, magazines, advice columns, newsletters and books, and on television, radio, and the Internet, you should be able to find plenty of guidance in managing your money without being totally dependent on a professional financial adviser. The trick is to keep your plan simple and clear. This is difficult for most people because they want to see finances as complex, and investing as an action-packed, competitive endeavour – they aim to mirror what they imagine traders do at their desks every day in and around the City.

A financial adviser is worth consulting if you need help in implementing a wealth-building and investment programme; if you want to begin investing but are unsure how to get started; if you own a number of diverse financial products but lack a coherent investment strategy; if you are worried about your retirement; or if you need advice about how to face a money crisis you don't know how to handle due to accumulated debt, unpaid taxes, divorce, bankruptcy or another emergency situation.

The first step is to find the right *kind* of financial adviser. There is a crucial distinction between an Independent Financial Adviser (IFA), who can recommend investment products offered by any company, and a tied agent, who sells products on behalf of a single company. By definition, the IFA is more likely to offer impartial investment advice than the tied agent, who will almost certainly recommend that you buy whatever investment products his company has to offer.

An IFA may earn a living in one of several ways. Some IFAs charge clients a flat fee or an hourly rate; others earn commissions on the sales of investment products. In the latter case, their advice *could* be biased towards investment vehicles that pay the best commission. Before hiring an IFA, be sure to ask about how he or she gets paid: knowing this will help you to evaluate the recommendations offered.

Generally speaking, a tied agent is useful if you've already done your research and decided you want a product from a specific company. The tied agent will then answer your questions, help you make the purchase, and submit the forms for you.

As I've said earlier, when you're considering hiring a financial adviser, it is best to arrange a face-to-face meeting. Bring with you a list of questions and a statement of your financial goals. Make sure the prospective adviser talks in a way you can understand and offers advice that is truly tailored to your needs. Above all, never be too embarrassed to ask for explanations. The adviser should be able to describe his or her recommendations in language anyone can understand.

Here are some questions to ask a prospective financial adviser:

- Do you deal in all the areas in which I want financial advice, such as retirement planning, saving, planning for university fees, etc?
- What will your fees be, including both initial charges and ongoing expenses? Is your income based on sales commissions on specific products?
- How long have you worked in this field? (Look for a track record of at least ten years, including experience in both bull and bear markets.)
- Have you had clients with backgrounds and goals similar to mine? How did you work with them?
- What makes you different from other financial advisers? (Watch out for braggarts, individuals who are a little too confident, and those who talk only about spectacular or 'risk-free' profits.)
- Have there been any customer complaints about you? (Don't be shy about asking this. The FSA website will give details if there have been any.)

- What licences do you have? Which professional organisations are you a member of? (Answers may include, at a personal level, Membership of the Chartered Institute of Securities and Investments, a Chartered Financial Planner (CFP) or the Institute for Financial Planning. The firm may be a member of the APCIMS, or CISI amongst others; however, the individual and the firm must be regulated by the Association of Solicitor Investment Managers and the Financial Services Authority, which will become the Financial Conduct Authority or FCA.)
- How frequently will you provide me with written reports? Can I call you on the phone with questions and concerns?

Make sure the prospective adviser is asking *you* the right questions as well. He or she should enquire about your long-term goals, your risk tolerance, your timetable, and how much you could afford to lose in a worst-case scenario. Be wary of an adviser who seems to offer 'one-size-fits-all' recommendations to every client.

A crucial word of caution: don't think that hiring a stockbroker or financial adviser means you can retire into the background and just send a cheque whenever your adviser recommends a new trade or security. Working with a broker or adviser is not a passive endeavour. You must be involved and informed. An investment professional may have enormous expertise, but he or she should communicate to you why a specific investment or strategy is appropriate for your specific combination of investment objectives and risk tolerance, and you must agree with his or her assessment. Remember, it's your money. Don't relinquish all of the decision-making power to somebody else. And if you are disappointed with what a broker has done with your investments, or are uncomfortable with what he or she has begun doing with them, it's time to leave and find another.

If you feel you've been treated inappropriately or illegally, you have the right to complain and seek action. Start by writing to the broker directly, outlining your grievance and indicating the amount you think you've lost as a result. If you don't receive the remedy you want from the initial letter, write to your adviser's Compliance Officers. All companies must have established procedures for handling complaints. If it is determined that your complaint is justified, then the company may try to settle the matter internally in order to keep you as a customer.

If you're still not satisfied, you should complain to the Financial Ombudsman Services (www.financial-ombudsman.org.uk). The FSA outlines the steps for making a complaint at its website: www.fsa.gov.uk/pages/consumerinformation/if_things_go_wrong/index.shtml.

The FSA also produces a leaflet called *Guide to Making a Complaint*, and they'll send you a copy if you phone 0800 917 3311. It is your right and you should exercise it when you need to. It is not fair to complain, for example, if an investment recommended in good faith by a broker or adviser loses money through unforeseeable circumstances; however, if you have been misled or lied to, you should certainly take action.

Your Portfolio

Whether it is your first time investing or you already have experience, here's an important principle to keep in mind: do not put all your eggs in one basket. This familiar warning holds true no matter how much money you have to invest.

If you have only a small amount to begin with, it is probably best that you limit your investment choices to a diversified unit trust or OEIC with a reasonable-to-low total expense ratio and a long history of delivering good, relatively steady returns. Buying shares of a pooled investment product gives you 1) access to the skills of an investment professional who selects the securities in which the unit trust or OEIC is invested; and 2) immediate diversification, because there are usually shares, bonds, or both of many companies held in the unit trust's or OEIC's portfolio.

If you have enough money to buy individual securities, you should strategically aim to create a portfolio that includes different asset classes, or different business sectors within each asset class. You are thus creating your own diversified portfolio. Think of diversification as an important risk-management strategy. You are protecting yourself from being overexposed to the risk of one company or one sector.

Deciding exactly how to diversify your investment portfolio is known as *asset allocation* and there are many ways to approach it using both individual securities (shares and bonds) and different types of unit trusts or OEICs. Today, most financial services firms offer guidance or overviews about allocation on their websites. More specific customised recommendations, including the percentages and specific investments in each asset class, are created following personal meetings with a broker or adviser after he or she has gathered key information about your financial situation and investment objectives.

Below are two classic asset allocation models that, I believe, can serve as useful guidelines. As you learn more about the markets and products (as well as your 'investment personality'), you can work alone or with a financial professional to create a customised model that works best for you. Keep in mind that the markets are dynamic – always moving and changing. You should occasionally review your allocation model to make sure it stays appropriate to your changing financial situation.

The three major asset classes are: shares, bonds and cash. *Cash* refers to savings in a bank or building society, which are very low risk. It can also be held in a cash ISA. It is important to think of how much immediate liquidity you want to keep available.

Shares and *bonds* have been explained in detail in previous chapters. Money invested in a unit trust or OEIC can fall into either the bonds or shares asset class, depending on the investments in the fund's portfolio.

Please note that I am not making any specific recommendations regarding the right asset allocation for you. The two models I've chosen to feature are widely used, but are being discussed here primarily to highlight points you might perhaps consider. Some basic measures for determining percentages in each asset class are: age, preservation of capital, need for current income, and whether your approach will be conservative or aggressive. The final choice of percentages is yours, always keeping in mind your own risk tolerance.

The Age-Adjusted Mix (variable)

An asset allocation model that many people like and find easy to follow is the Age-Adjusted Mix. Its formula is designed to change your investment mix from focusing on capital growth in your early years to a more conservative approach whose objective is preservation of capital as you grow older. The formula is:

100% minus Your Age =   Percentage of Assets Invested in Shares or Fund That Invest in Shares

The remaining percentage would be invested in bonds (or a mixture of bonds and low risk cash). So, when you are 30 years old, 100% minus your age would result in an allocation of 70% of your investment money to equities and 30% to bonds. [Remember: Funds can be used instead of individual securities.] When you reach 50, you would have 50% in stocks and 50% in high-grade bonds. You would adjust the percentage each year, typically on your birthday or at the beginning of the calendar year. Rebalancing the percentages once a year enables the investor to capture some of the capital gains made on shares and invest that money in more conservative bonds in which he or she would earn interest. If bonds have outperformed equities by the rebalancing date, then an investor would move some of the gains made on fixed-income securities into more growth- or income-producing equities.

The important benefit of this allocation model is that it serves as a reminder that you should periodically look at where you are in your life cycle, examine what changes have occurred, see what is happening in the investment markets, and adjust your holdings or your strategy appropriately.

The Conservative or Balanced Mix (40% bonds, 60% shares)

This allocation model has preservation of capital as one of its goals; hence, the high percentage in bonds. It seeks to provide both steady income (from the interest paid on the bonds) while offering some opportunity for capital appreciation, depending on the types of stocks or funds that complete the remainder of the portfolio. It is important to rebalance this allocation annually. If shares have grown more in value, you sell them and invest the capital gains in lower-risk bonds. If bonds have outperformed stocks, then you sell off some of the bonds and use the profits to buy shares that may be temporarily undervalued and getting ready to rise in price. With this allocation one is unlikely to be either the biggest winner or, perhaps most importantly, the biggest loser. When cash is factored into this conservative blend, the allocation looks as follows: 55% equities, 35% bonds, 10% cash.

Generally speaking, the more aggressive an investor wants to be, the more money would be invested in shares, especially those that are more growth-oriented. A conservative investor, concerned about preservation of capital, would invest more in high-grade bonds or, if he or she were a little more risk-tolerant, in blue-chip stocks. Both approaches have their obvious advantages and disadvantages. The more conservative an investment approach, the greater the impact of inflation will be over the long-term, reducing the purchasing power of your money. A more growth-oriented approach offers the opportunity for greater gains, but is subject to more volatility and risk of loss.

Deciding on an asset allocation model or strategy gives you the broad outline of your investment plan. Your next step is to choose the specific shares, bonds, unit trusts or OEICs that will constitute your investment portfolio. Start with what interests you – a specific company, a business sector, a part of the world, or a type of security. You don't have to invest your real money immediately. Follow it on paper as a paper investment first to get a sense of how the investment is affected by economic forces, as well as the day-to-day movement of the stock market. Once you actually invest, the learning process will naturally accelerate. With 'skin in the game', you'll be motivated to learn more, to know more. Below are some useful tips to keep in mind throughout your journey as an investor in the stock market.

- *Focus on a limited number of companies.* Few people have the time or energy to keep tabs on more than a dozen or so companies spread across a variety of industry sectors. Keep your portfolio simple enough so that you can periodically (weekly, monthly, or quarterly) review all your holdings within a reasonable amount of time.
- *Invest over time.* Don't feel the need to invest all of your money at one time. If you do invest all at one time, you will certainly have the potential to make a big gain; however, you could also make a big loss. Perhaps a more prudent approach is to invest modest amounts of money at regular intervals as the market moves up and down. You get the benefits of pound-cost averaging, which means your money buys more shares or units when prices are low.
- *Core-and-explore* is a good strategy for the conservative investor interested in preserving his or her capital, devoting small amounts of money to investment in interesting growth areas. The strategy is simple: Put the majority (the 'core') of your money into an established, large-cap or index unit trust,

exchange-traded fund or an OEIC. Use the remainder of your capital to 'explore' investment in individual companies or sectors that are more growth-oriented – such as mid-cap stock or foreign companies. But first, ask yourself how you would feel if you lost your 'exploring' money. Could you cope with the loss emotionally? If not, reduce the amount of money you allocated to the growth part of your portfolio.

- *Pay attention to market trends.* As you recall, a bull market is a period of investor optimism, when the market as a whole is rising and most companies follow suit. When the bulls are running, buy shares across a broad spectrum of sectors and ride the buoyant market. By contrast, a bear market is a time of pessimism, when most shares drift downward in value. When a bear market strikes, wait on the sidelines and keep your money in cash and short-term liquid securities.

- *Consider using a stop-loss system.* This means establishing a price *below* the purchase price at which you will sell your shares. For example, suppose you buy shares at £12 each. You might decide to set a stop-loss price of £9 per share. (You must instruct your broker to place the sell-stop order.) Thus, the *most* you can possibly lose on your purchase is £3 per share. The advantage of this system is that it takes the influence of emotion out of your selling decisions, preventing you from holding on to securities as they plummet further and further while you say to yourself, 'Surely it'll turn around soon,' or, 'It's certainly going to hit the bottom by next week.' You might also set a high at which you will sell, or 'take profits'.

- *Decide to sell the same way you decided to buy.* When pondering whether or not to sell shares, try to forget about what you paid for them and ask yourself: 'Knowing what I know about this company, would I buy these shares today at the current price?' If the answer is 'no', sell them, no matter whether you will make a loss or a profit by doing so.

• *Recoup your original investment and let your profits run.* Once your securities have increased in value, you may want to sell off enough to recoup the original amount you invested and then let your profits continue to make money for you. For example, suppose your original investment of £2,000 in a fund or company's shares has grown in value to £5,000. You could sell off enough of the security to get back the £2,000 you originally paid. [Note: Some conservative investors deposit this money into a high-interest savings account.] After the sale, you will still own £3,000 of the securities. If the price continues to appreciate, you'll make money on your profits.

• *Learn from your mistakes.* Whenever you lose money on an investment, don't immediately reinvest the money. Take some time to reflect. Ask yourself what lessons you can learn from the mishap. Did you get carried away and take on a level of risk that exceeds what you were prepared for? Were you dabbling in an industry sector that you didn't know enough about? Did you ignore warning signs because you were overly focused on the gains you believed you would make instead of the possibility of loss? Did you ignore what you felt in your gut or intuition? No one is smart enough or lucky enough to have winning trades 100% of the time. Your goal should be to have more profitable transactions than losing ones. Make a point of learning a lesson from every transaction – those on which you make money and those on which you lose money –

and you'll keep getting smarter – intellectually and intuitively – as an investor.

- *Always Consider Inflation Risk in Your Strategy.* Inflation silently and perniciously undermines the value of your savings and investment because, like far too many people, you probably fail to think about it when formulating your investment strategy. How much purchasing power do you think the pound made in 1971 would have today? A little less than 9p! Now imagine the effect that inflation could have on your money over your lifetime, which I hope will be longer than the 40-year example I just used. Of course, the long-term rate of inflation cannot be accurately predicted. But it is, nonetheless, a number you need to keep in mind when determining the asset allocation mix of your portfolio. If the rate of inflation is 5%, for example, how much pre-tax return do you need on your investment so that your money maintains its purchasing power? The answer is 6.25%. And you would have to save or reinvest the gains, not spend them. Now think about the rate you're getting on your savings account or the interest that is being paid on gilts in today's low interest rate environment. Realistically, this means that some of your money probably should be invested in equities that have good, consistent dividend yields. Stocks with this characteristic are blue-chip and income shares and they tend to be less volatile than other types of equities, and the dividends can help your money keep pace with inflation. In the final analysis, keeping inflation risk in mind will help you determine the asset allocation mix and associate volatility risk that will help you protect the value of your money.

Summary

I hope this book has helped you discover why understanding the stock market is an essential element in successful investing as well as an essential element to understanding the economy and the how money works. As you've seen, the stock market serves two main purposes. First, it enables businesses and other organisations to raise capital. This is the money they need to improve, expand, and grow. Second, the stock market enables the investors who provide that capital to participate in the growth of those enterprises. As a business grows, so does the value of its ordinary shares, the reliability of its dividend payments on all of its equities, and the dependability of the interest payments on its bonds. Investors who own the organisation's securities directly or through funds benefit as their net worth and financial security increases.

But as you've also learned, the opportunity for income and growth from investing comes with risks. Any investment – whether a blue chip stock, a high-grade bond, or a diversified fund – has the potential of making money for you, or losing it either through a decline in price or as a result of inflation. You have to decide, either alone or with the help of a professional, whether investing is for you. And if it is, you must then decide what investment products you will use to participate in the financial markets and how much risk you're willing to tolerate in exchange for the possibility of making your money grow.

The direct connection between risk and reward is the single most essential truth about the stock market as well as other investment markets. Getting the balance between the two correct for yourself and your investment objectives is an ongoing challenge. It is also ever-changing as individual companies, business sectors, governments, and the overall economy go through different cycles.

But there is another aspect of the stock market that I was surprised to discover when I began working on Wall Street. Even after nearly 30 years of working in the investment markets, this fact continues to amaze and motivate me. The financial markets are places where creativity flourishes. They are dynamic – continually evolving, especially technologically, and constantly introducing not only new stock and bond offerings, each representing a potentially innovative and exciting new business concept, but entirely new investment products and ideas. This steady stream of fresh ideas is a natural outgrowth of the nature of capitalism, and each successful one (as well as some of those that failed) has helped build the prosperous, technologically advanced society we live in today.

The genius of the stock market is that it gives people like you and me a place where we can, if we choose, participate in business creativity – both its potential rewards and its risks. Investing in shares, bonds, funds, and other types of securities is not for everybody. But for millions of people who choose as part of a diversified financial strategy to allocate part of their earnings or savings to investing, the stock market is one of the most powerful tools we have to achieve our long-term investment objectives, to build financial security – in short, to make our money grow and retains its value.

List of Key Abbreviations and Acronyms

AGM – Annual General Meeting
AIF – Authorised Investment Fund
AMC – Annual Management Charge
AUT – Authorised Investment Trust
Bps – Basis point
BV – Book Value
Capex – Capital Expenditure
CGT – Capital Gains Tax
COGS – Cost of Goods Sold
Conv – Convertible
CPI – Consumer Prices Index
CROCI – Cash Return on Capital Invested
CTA – Commodity Trading Adviser
Cum Pref – Cumulative Preference
CUSIP – The Committee on Uniform Securities Identification Procedures
CVOL – Cumulative Volume
CY – Current Year
DCF – Discounted Cash Flow
DJIA – Dow Jones Industrial Average
DPS – Dividend per Share
DY – Dividend Yield
EBIT – Earnings before Interest and Tax

EBITDA – Earnings before Interest, Tax, Depreciation and Amortisation

EGM – Extraordinary General Meeting

EMS – Exchange Market Size

EPS – Earnings per Share

Est – Estimate

ETC – Exchange Traded Commodity

ETF – Exchange Traded Fund

EV/EBIT – Enterprise Value/ Earnings before Interest and Tax

EV/EBITDA – Enterprise Value/ Earnings before Interest, Tax, Depreciation and Amortisation

EV/Sales – Enterprise Value/Sales

FCA – Financial Conduct Authority

FCF – Free Cash Flow

FSA – Financial Services Authority

FY – Financial Year

GDP – Gross Domestic Product

GRY – Gross Redemption Yield

H1/2 – 1st Half/2nd Half

Hist – Historic

IFRS – International Financial Reporting Standards

IHT – Inheritance Tax

ISA – Individual Savings Account

ISIN – International Securities Identification Number

KIID – Key Investor Information Document

LfL – Like for Like

L/S – Long/Short

LSE – London Stock Exchange (also London School of Economics)

LTM – Last twelve months

MiFID – Markets in Financial Instruments Directive

MLRO – Money Laundering Reporting Officer

MTF – Multilateral Trading Facility
NASDAQ – National Association of Securities Dealers
    Automated Quotation System
NAV – Net Asset Value
NMS – Normal Market Size
NRY – Net Redemption Yield
NY – Next Year
NYSE – New York Stock Exchange
OEIC – Open Ended Investment Company
OTC – Over the Counter
P/BV – Price/Book value
PAT – Profit After Tax
PBT – Profit Before Tax
PEG – Price to Earnings/Growth
PER – Price to Earnings Ratio
PIBS – Permanent Interest Bearing Shares
PRA – Prudential Regulation Authority
Pref – Preference or Preferred
Pros – Prospective
PTP – Pre-Tax Profit
Q1/2/3/4 – 1st, 2nd, 3rd and 4th Quarter
RIE – Recognised Investment Exchange
RNS – Regulatory News Service
ROA – Return on Assets
ROCE – Return on Capital Employed
ROE – Return on Equity
RPI – Retail Prices Index
RSP – Retail Service Provider
S&P – Standard & Poor's
SEDOL – Stock Exchange Daily Official List
SG&A – Selling, General & Administrative Expense IFRS
SIPP – Self Invested Personal Pension
Std Dev – Standard Deviation

TER – Total Expense Ratio
TSC – Treasury Select Committee
UCITS – Undertaking for Collective Investments in Transferable Securities
VWAP Volume Weighted Average Price
XD – Ex Dividend
YOY – Year on Year
ZCB – Zero Coupon Bond
ZDP – Zero Dividend Preference Share

INDEX

Bold = Key term – see text for full explanation

exchange-traded commodities
(ETCs) 157, 173
exchange-traded funds (ETFs)
20, 49, 148, 157, 168–73
execution-only broking firms
41–2, 43–4, 178–80
expansion, economic phase
64, 65, 79
expense ratios *see* total
expense ratios (TERs)

face value 112, 113, 135, 140
see also nominal value; par
value; principal
family of funds 150
Federal Reserve Bank 143
fees 7, 42, 116, 141, 149, 154,
156, 158, 161–3, 167–8,
180–3, 187
see also commission
financial advisers 2, 11–13,
110–11, 161, 177, 183–90
financial crisis (2011–12) 1,
8, 10, 112
Financial Services Authority
(FSA) 18, 19, 20, 45, 167,
187, 189
Financial Times (FT) 17,
57–8, 100, 118, 126, 146,
158–9, 164
Fitch 131, 135, 136, 137
fixed-income securities 71–2,
74, 78, 96, 112–47
see also bonds; gilts
flag formations 105

floatation *see* initial public
offerings (IPOs)
floaters 114–15
forward pricing 159, 164
Franklin, Benjamin 14
FTSE indices 17, 58, 63, 168
FTSE 100 index 69, 87, 89,
96, 100–1, 102–4, 134,
167–8, 174
FTSE 250 index 100–1, 152
FTSE All-Share index 101,
134, 168–9
FTSE Small Cap index 101
fully diluted EPS 83, 84
fundamental analysis 80–1,
111
funds
investing in 148–74
tracker 96, 153, 168–70,
172, 174–5
see also exchange-traded
funds
futures 9

Gilt Edge Market Makers
(GEMMs) 125
gilts 45, 96, 114, 121, 124,
137, 145, 183, 197
conventional 126–8
index-linked 125–6, 128,
129
stripped 129
undated 128–9
global events, impact of on
markets 80